Adventures of a South Sea Missionary

F. Edward Butterworth

Adventures of a South Sea Missionary

HERALD HOUSE, Independence, Missouri
1961

Preface

At the age of twenty-six, F. Edward Butterworth and his bride of a few months made their first trip to the South Pacific as missionaries for the Reorganized Church of Jesus Christ of Latter Day Saints. That was in 1944. Since that time they have made two other missionary tours of French Polynesia, the latest ending in 1958.

Out of the experiences of approximately nine years in this faraway mission of the church, Brother Butterworth has recorded some of the more fascinating ones in this book. Much of this material first appeared in serial form in the youth magazine, *Stride*. Because of general interest, it is now made available as a book—with many new photos and some additional material.

"Eddie," as he is best known, has a very interesting style of writing. He keeps his readers in suspense as he describes his shipwreck, the finding of the Kon-Tiki, pearl diving and spearfishing, meeting Tahitian royalty, native customs, and walking in a fire pit.

As this book is published, F. Edward Butterworth is serving as a missionary in the United States. But who knows, he may soon be serving again among his many Polynesian friends halfway around the world! Whenever the call comes, Eddie and his wife and three children will be ready to go and to serve.

Paul A. Wellington
Book Editor

Contents

Chapter 1

The author at his desk in Tahiti

Beautiful Tahiti

The submarine nets were secretly opened and our small Norwegian cargo vessel, "Thor I," zigzagged a predetermined course out of the San Francisco harbor.

All the precautions of survival had been rehearsed and were now in the process of execution. Silently, majestically onward we glided toward Tahiti, the island paradise in the heart of the South Pacific.

The fury of World War II had moved into the Pacific, and we were required to pass through a fringe of the war area. Enemy subs and floating mines were an ever lurking danger, especially at night, for the magic of radar was no part of our meager equipment.

Our limited baggage was carefully customs inspected at San Francisco. All written and printed documents were carefully inspected and officially sealed up inside my brief case to be opened only by the Inspector de Police at Papeete.

It was dusk as we looked backward toward the hazy outline of the California coast. We were invited into the lounge for *aperitifs* to whet the appetite for our first meal at sea and to get acquainted with the other passengers. Actually we had little appetite due to the excitement of leaving the mainland and the roll of the ship, but we did manage to sip some chilled fruit juice and mince on sugared cookies.

We had a very interesting group of passengers. The rotund Mr. Ball was owner of a large glass manufacturing company and his famous name was molded on most of the glass jars being exported to Tahiti on the "Thor I." He and his attractive wife owned an island villa and made regular trips to Tahiti at the end of each fiscal year. They were a very pleasant elderly couple and we became close friends during our stay in Tahiti.

Fritz was a small, energetic American who was returning to his native *vahine* in his adopted country after a brief trip to the States. He had come to Frisco for several crates of purebred baby chicks to develop a sturdy breed of chickens in the islands. We later benefited from his good venture but were not too happy at the time, since he was nursing them in his cabin next to ours. We admired him for his ability to converse with our Tahitian steward and several of the Tahitian sailors, for despite the good tutoring of Apostle Clyde F. Ellis, we found the language still an unintelligible blur.

Mr. Taran was another wandering American who owned a recreation hall and small hotel in Papeete. There were twelve passengers in all—the absolute quota for this small cargo ship.

At the table we had a place of honor at the captain's left which made it very embarrassing when we did not show up at the dining room. However, after we adjusted to the roll of the ship we seldom missed a meal.

The first night out was unusually black. This was accentuated by the fact that we were under strict blackout orders from the Defense Department. Lilly Raye and I were typical landlubbers invariably referring to "above and below" as "upstairs and downstairs." We had not even noticed the important bulletin board where vital announcements and news items were posted daily. We came to regret this later when we were rudely shocked out of an afternoon siesta by the blasting tremors of machine-gun fire from both rear and forward emplacements.

"Enemy Attack"

With hardly a thought of my bride of only a few months, I hit the upper deck two steps at a time to investigate the crisis. Everyone seemed to be scurrying to their lifeboat positions, pulling on life jackets. The spitting machine guns drowned out the blaring intercom instructions. I watched for a few seconds as the strafing bullets made a pattern in the sea beginning at shipside and working outward suggesting that we had encountered a pack of enemy subs.

Blazing distress signals bursting high overhead looked like bombs. I rushed back to our quarters where Lilly Raye was hurriedly dressing and added to the confusion by announcing an enemy attack. Within seconds we were on deck nursing our worries, the least of which was that our life jackets were on backward.

It was some time before we could realize that this was only a routine wartime drill which had been duly posted in advance on the bulletin board.

A cruise of sixteen days such as this can be very dull to a person who is not a lover of the sea. Without swimming pool or adequate library entertainment we had to seek other outlets for our pent-up energy as the days wore on. Our promenading on the small deck simulated the antics of caged animals.

Blue Ocean, Silver Moon

We finally discovered an interesting diversion in studying the restless sea and the atmosphere around us. We were fascinated by the changing colors, the incidence of flying fish, and at night the flashing phosphorescence which appeared when small white-caps charged up from the dark ocean. Being blacked out, the friction of the boat moving through the water stirred the phosphorus and at the water-line showed like a streak of fire as we slithered along on moonless nights.

As we neared Tahiti, we noticed the quickening pristine clarity of the tropical atmosphere. Billowing crystalline clouds became more apparent as we steamed steadily onward. Rays from the sunrises and sunsets began to show that there was a gradual thinning of the upper dust, and the prismatic delineation of the spectrum became more and more striking in brilliant hues.

We watched the familiar Big Dipper drop into the ocean and in a few days were able to identify the Southern Cross, bringing impressively to mind that we were entering a strange and distant world. We were now far below the equator, and there was little fuss as we crossed the famous imaginary line. On larger steamers it would have been a gala occasion with Neptune and a colorful array of costumed gods and goddesses dunking the uninitiated.

Never before had we seen the moon so silvery and bright. The clarity of moonlight was sufficient to permit reading quite comfortably. Although we had no d'stinct objects to measure depth except the illusory ethereal formations, distances seemed to shrink as we neared Tahiti. The opalescence of the changing horizon was magnificent.

Beautiful Tahiti

It was early Sunday morning, November 12, 1944, when we met with the most arresting sight the human eye can perceive. Out of the dark-blue ocean a beautiful green sleeping giant slowly arose. We shall never forget the sight. This was Tahiti, the pearl of the Pacific.

We came nearer and nearer, and soon the outline of houses and the detail of coconut palms were clearly visible. A predominance of cyclists with only an occasional automobile was indeed a contrast to the world of wheels we had left. Soon the first island sounds greeted our ears—the bark of a dog,

13

roosters' crowing, and finally man's own crude invention, the automobile horn.

No one was expecting us, for during wartime the movement of ships had to be kept secret. Even cablegrams were not allowed. However, President Frederick M. Smith had written words of encouragement to Seventy J. Charles May, who had been isolated at Tahiti for several years because of the war. The letter did not state exactly when we would arrive, but Brother and Sister May watched each approaching ship anxiously in hopes of receiving news of a successor.

"That's J. Charles May"

The "Thor I" was met by the pilot boat just outside the reef near an enormous pass. We were informed that all large ships are piloted into the Papeete lagoon by experienced pilots because of the stones jutting here and there from the floor of the pass.

The pale lagoon was peaceful and in sharp contrast to the deep color of the open sea to which we had become accustomed. The shallow sand bottom showed like powdered jade through the clear rippling waters as we inched gently along. From her basket-shaped harbor, the capital city, Papeete, had drawn its pretty name—"Pape" means water and "ete" means basket.

The wharf was jammed with inquisitive brown-skinned natives pressing a sprinkling of white foreign element into a colorful pattern. To fa-

Three veteran missionaries to French Polynesia: Allen J. Breckenridge, J. Charles May, and F. Edward Butterworth

cilitate landing formalities the pilot boat had also brought the customs and police on board to check our hand luggage and landing papers before we docked.

When we were finally ready to go ashore there was a tingling of anticipation as we found our places along the top railing of the ship. Mr. Taran pointed out a short pleasant-faced man surrounded by a group of grinning natives. "That's Mr. J. Charles May," he said helpfully, for we had never formally met our predecessor whom we had come to relieve. Almost simultaneously our hands and his shot up in a gesture of greeting and welcome.

Natives whom we had never seen before were smiling and waving vigorously. It was hard to keep

15

A view of the Papeete harbor

back the tears. The gangplank was soon in place and a young native, Tautu Samuela, bounded up to greet us in broken English. He picked up our baggage and motioned for us to follow him.

We stepped ashore and planted our feet firmly on the shores to which we had been sent by General Conference appointment. We were literally being crushed in the crowd of friends who wanted to shake hands and put the traditional *hei* of welcome around our necks.

The Center of Attention

Brother May finally reached us through the pressing throng, and I recall slipping my arm around his shoulder without uttering a word. The lump in my throat made it impossible to audibly express the joy of meeting Latter Day Saints in such a distant and primitive mission field. We had arrived in Polynesia where, centuries before the discovery of the Pacific, sun-bronzed Vikings cruised up and down the long Pacific swells in curious ocean-going craft, visiting the palm-studded islands.

We were not favorably impressed with the rambling shack city of Papeete as we drove slowly down the narrow main street past a quaint row of old-fashioned and unpainted frame buildings. This did not correspond with our first storybook impressions of Tahiti.

We were heading north away from the main section of Papeete, followed by a large group of jabbering natives who must have been discussing our clothes from the way they were gesturing. We were certainly the center of attention.

Tarona

When we had gone the equivalent of about three city blocks the road turned sharply to the right and the white sea wall surrounding our large church compound came into view. This was Tarona, rising like an oasis from the contrasting surroundings. The yard was fringed with native frame dwellings built on cement stilts to protect them from frequent floods.

The driver pulled up in front of a large canopy-type assembly building near the center of the com-

Street scene in Papeete, Tahiti

19

pound just back of the church. We were escorted to the front door of an impressively large frame church building.

The flowers around our necks were stifling hot, and the sweet odor along with the nervous strain of the experience had a slight sickening effect upon us. As we stepped up to the front door we noticed for the first time that it was full of people. We had nearly forgotten this was Sunday morning.

Horahitu

As we walked down the aisle the members arose and burst forth in a familiar and full-voiced hymn. We were thrilled beyond expression though we could not understand a word they were saying. We were seated on two homemade chairs on the rostrum and through a film of tears of joy tried to drink in the color of this very impressive service.

Horahitu, whose name was familiar to us, stretched to his full six-foot height and began to speak in a very oratorical manner. We were impressed with the fluency with which he spoke but did not notice that his eyes were closed. He was engaged in prayer, but not an eye of the congregation was closed, nor had the members ceased to look at us since we entered the room.

Following the lengthy prayer of thanksgiving for protection over us on our journey, they filed by, piling on still more flowers and pressing crumpled francs into our hands. We were taken on a short walk around the compound with Brother May translating for me and Sister Letha May translating for Lilly Raye.

It was a beautiful yard reaching one short city block across the front and nearly the same along the side. After a while the deacon tugged at a well-worn rope dangling from the bell tower of the Tarona church and sounded out a curious call to worship.

We had the feeling that we had journeyed into the past. This was the beginning of our South Sea Island missionary adventure.

Chapter 2

A copra schooner

Storm at Sea

"Tohora! Tohora!"

The excited shout announced the appearance of a whale spouting high off the starboard bow of our tiny copra schooner.

The captain signaled the helmsman to spin the tiller toward the sea monster whose gleaming body was breaking surface in slow rhythmic motion.

Lilly Raye and I were so engrossed in the thrill of our first sight of a whale we completely overlooked recording the incident on film. We seemed to be about to ram into the whale, but actually we were still some distance away.

"Tupohe!" the captain shouted. His voice came from high up on the ship's rigging. He was signaling for the motors to be cut off. He had one leg wound around the rope ladder leading to the top of the mast and was taking aim with a small bore rifle. Almost simultaneously with the stopping of the motors, several large fins appeared in quick succession and the tail flippers broke high out of the water indicating a dive to safer waters. The crack of rifle fire seemed insignificant indeed against such an exhibition of animal power and the protecting shield of whale blubber. The captain

ordered the ship on its original course and came to the rail where we had been watching.

"Is that the first *tohora* you have seen, *Edua ma?*" The captain blew the smoke from the barrel of his rifle.

"The very first," we admitted. "It was a beautiful sight, but did you expect to kill it with that small bore rifle?"

"I always take a shot at them if I can get close enough," the captain explained. "If I happen to hit a vital organ the whale will eventually die and wash up on some near-by *motu.*"

The captain's words were to echo and re-echo many times after that when we discovered large vertebrae or whales' teeth on the many atolls we subsequently visited during our half-score years in French Polynesia. A dead whale discovered on the beach will bring a considerable income to the finder, depending of course upon the amount and color of wax-oil which can be retrieved, to say nothing of the other collectors' items such as teeth and the useful whalebone.

It was nearly dusk and the passengers on the "Florence" had settled back almost to normal. Lilly Raye and I were making our first trip away from Tahiti to visit the Tuamotuan Archipelago, the famed "South Sea Islands." We were the only *popaa* among approximately twenty-five natives, all bedded down under a low flapping canvas. Our pandanus sleeping mats were fishboned along both slopes of the stern deck.

"It certainly is stormy," I said. "Could that gale be the gentle trade wind we've read so much about?" Lilly Raye was in no mood to joke, as she was already beginning to show a little green around the gills.

Seasick

"Do you want to go below?" I asked.

"I'd rather be drenched than to suffocate in that hot bunk, and furthermore I can't stand cockroaches running over my face." There was a tinge of finality in her tone.

Actually I was glad she didn't want to go below. I was feeling a little squeamish myself. The storm gradually increased and the ship began to pitch at seemingly precarious angles, then roll in sequence to almost the same opposite degree. A very little of this lurching is enough to create a churning effect on a landlubber's stomach. The noisy battening down activities suggested we were in for a bad night.

Our good friend, Captain Ioane Gabral, tolled out six bells on the piercing *oe* just above our heads.

"*Edua,* I think you and *Lili Re* had better go below."

"Are we in for a serious storm?" I tried not to betray any sign of fear in this question.

"Nothing to worry about," he consoled. "But it will be better *i raro.*"

Trying not to appear seasick, I forced myself up on my elbows and wheezed out an excuse for not

The Mariposa, luxury liner. How the author wished he were on it.

complying. Pointing meaningfully at Lilly Raye, who was covered up stork fashion, and wagging my head with a "you know" air, I said, "Seasick! The copra fumes below are too pungent for her."

"You look a little sick yourself, *Edua*," he laughed. Up to that time, I thought I had covered up pretty well, but now that my secret was known it didn't take much to convince me I was really sick. I didn't quite make it to the elusive rail, but I will say this in my own defense, few are any more efficient on the mop-up.

"Let me give you a little advice," the captain said, shifting his weight as the ship rocked. "Don't fight the movement of the ship. That's the main reason a person gets all tied up inside. Instead of pulling back to keep the ship from turning over, try to turn her over."

"Too many people doing that already," I stuttered, convinced that I was right. I looked around to see how the natives were making out. Most of them were just as sick as we were, but they, too, were making the mistake of bracing themselves against each roll. Those who were relaxed and rolling from side to side in motion were spared the agony of seasickness.

Unfortunately the captain did not convince us we should go below, so he had our bunk mattresses brought up from below and shoved them under us as an insulation against the rock-hard deck which was beating us black and blue.

Within a few hours the boat was all but out of control, it seemed to us. The seas were tremendous. Each wave rocked us high, charging under us with merciless force. As we nosed into the next wave our stern propeller was exposed, causing a terrific strain on our motor as it revved out of control. We would then drop heavily into the trough as the ship shuddered and skidded from the shock of the screw taking hold again, driving us aimlessly into the black night.

The captain was right—we should have gone below, but he was too busy keeping the ship headed into the storm to look after the passengers now. We were on our own. With some difficulty we made for the gangway and tried to get below. Excited commands, yelling, and crying of women and children as they stumbled around on the deck were very disconcerting. We finally made it, half stumbling and half crawling into the dining room.

Down Below

The sliding door was forced shut as the waves were now breaking regularly over the decks. It was stifling inside, but the muffled noise was at least more comforting. An elderly native woman, half sobbing of fright, told us this was the worst storm she had ever seen and begged us to use our influence with the captain (he was a member of the church) to return to Tahiti. We told her that the captain knew what was best for us and that we could best help him by offering a silent prayer.

The ship rocked at such precarious angles the ordinary blocks would not hold the dishes, pans, and glasses in the racks. We braced ourselves on the dining room benches and closed our eyes. Loose pans were banging around the room. Dishes crashed occasionally, and silverware was everywhere. This continued for several hours in a most severe manner, then seemed to fall into a pattern of rising and falling with an occasional shocking jolt throughout the night.

A Giant Elevator

The next day found us still afloat, but not out of danger by any means. The wind was high and the spray actually stung our flesh.

"How far are we from land?" I asked hopefully.

"Can't tell," the captain answered. "We aren't making much headway but are obliged to keep her nose in that direction." He pointed toward a series of gigantic waves rushing head on toward us. With the benefit of daybreak we were now aware of the imminent danger we faced and the terrific storm we had passed through during the night. Normally the Kaukura run took about twenty-four hours, but that was long since behind us and still no land was in sight.

The ship seemed to be speeding forward, but actually we were not gaining much due to the resistance of the sea. Sometimes as we dropped into the watery troughs we seemed to be surrounded by water on every side for a few seconds, then like a giant elevator the sea would carry us high giving us considerable visibility of a deserted and frenzied sea. At this precise moment we had a thrilling sensation as we seemed momentarily to be conquering the sea; but that feeling lasted only a few seconds, for as the liquid mountain charged under us it spilled us recklessly into the trough, skidding the stern half the length of the ship. The two helmsmen knew exactly when and how to spin the tiller.

"Aiiiiiii! Haere! Taviri!" and other exclamatory words followed every lurch of the ship. Sliced batten lines indicated that some freight had been abandoned during the night. The "if's" now began to crowd into our minds. What if the ancient diesel motor would stall? What if the termite-ridden rudder would break? What if the rusty hinge pins would come loose? These thoughts, however, were quickly forced out of mind as we uttered a silent prayer for protection.

A Threatening Cough

No one had eaten since the storm had begun and it was nearly noon. All morning long the captain had been below with the mechanic, nursing the motor along as it had developed a threatening cough. The thick haze which had darkened the sky for so long began slowly to dispel, and it seemed that the sun wanted to break through occasionally. We were evidently moving out of the storm area. Even the sea seemed more friendly, although visibly no change had taken place.

*One of our churches, on the island of
Kaukura in Tuamotuan Archipelago*

Captain Gabral finally appeared on deck from below and announced comfortingly, *"Ua Ora Tatou!"*

The bilge pump had clogged and the entire crew had been busy brigade fashion dumping bilge water. The pump was now in working order again and the motor was evidently all right.

The crew soon began a thorough cleanup of the battered ship. In the dining room, the native steward had to step over several prostrate forms including that of my wife who had hardly moved for twelve hours. Neither Lilly Raye nor I could take even a minimum of nourishment. The pungent odor of copra and diesel fumes along with the sight of seasick people all around us had taken our appetites

31

for sure. Nor did the sickening smell of greasy pork and boiling rice help the situation either.

I thought if I could just suck on a cool lemon it would cut the dark brown taste in my mouth. I suggested this to Lilly Raye, more to see if she was still among the living than anything else. Her answer, neither immediate nor audible, was, however, absolutely clear. She slowly pulled back the *tifaifai* covering her face, shuddered from the shoulders up, bloated her cheeks, turned over and slowly covered up again.

On the Horizon

I watched the steward wash the dishes without water by simply wiping them as clean as possible with a dry rag and replacing them in their racks. This didn't help the appetite either for any subsequent meal.

*Tahitian harbor showing
mountainous background*

"Fenua! Fenua!"
"Teihea?"
"Tera i mua e mea teitei roa!"

This announcement of the sight of land was the most welcome sound we had heard on the entire voyage. I lost all sense of seasickness immediately and stumbled to the deck expecting to see coconuts from the near-by trees about to drop on the deck. The sight was disappointing. It was still a deserted sea of charging waves as far as the eye could see.

"Where is the land?" I asked a native sailor.

"Tera i mua," he gestured vaguely ahead.

I strained to see, but despite an unusually good eyesight for distance, not a sign of land could I detect. I was scanning the horizon just a little below the cloud line, thinking to see the land rising high out of the water.

"I can't see a thing," I complained.

"You're looking too high," the sailor said helpfully. "It appears to be about this high and you can't see that until we are lifted high on the wave."

His measurement seemed to me to be about an inch high. This was enough to send me back to my pallet below very discouraged. At our snail's pace it would be several hours before we would arrive, and I didn't think either Lilly Raye or I could hold out that long. But the most disconcerting thing was the fact that we would be arriving at nightfall and would have to go over the vicious reef in semidarkness.

Chapter 3

Over the reef

Over the Reef

Kaukura is a typical atoll fringe with graceful coconut palms pushing up from decomposed coral soil. Unlike the volcanic mountainous islands, the atolls are built up of coral polyps which have lived and died, casting their shells into a common grave. After centuries of building up they finally reached the surface to form a coral barrier reef.

Stated simply, that portion above water became vegetated and finally inhabited. It was Captain Cook who discovered Kaukura in A.D. 1774, and now, 170 years later, we were about to make a landing on this beautiful island.

Fortunately the captain did not try a night landing. We circled the rim of the reef and headed for the protected side of the island where we could drop anchor for the night. The low island was now silhouetted against the crescent moon and radiated with a warmth of welcome. As we passed by, not a light was to be seen along the entire coast. The smooth waters indicated we had reached the point desired, so in order to steady the ship the anchor was dropped. We could not hope to have it reach bottom some half mile or so below us. For some time we sat beholding the peaceful little island, but the gentle rocking of the boat soon lulled us to sleep before the yellow crescent moon dropped into the restless sea.

It was the chug-chug of the familiar diesel motors which aroused us from the first good night's rest we had had since leaving Tahiti. The sun was a very comforting sight after such a stormy and harrowing voyage. We were again fringing the reef, heading back into the rougher waters approaching the so-called pass.

The reef is actually a colorful living stone and in the morning light showed a brilliant red as the churning surf receded. There were razor-sharp coral fingers covered with a poisonous film of fungus on the outer surface, ready to slash the unwary intruder. It is not unusual to see an occasional dorsal fin of a man-eating shark break water along the reef. The *Nohu* stone fish lurking in perfect camouflage along the reef has a poison stinger as fearsome and deadly as the fang of a serpent. These were just a few of the dangers awaiting us as we prepared to go ashore.

The "pass" is actually just a narrow, irregular crack in the reef. In some respects it appears to be the most dangerous place to go ashore, but if the boatswain is skilled with the rudder oar he can use the pass to advantage during low tide. In high tide one can go ashore nearly anywhere along the reef. Everyone seemed to be in high spirits at the prospects of going ashore. Having slept, minced breakfast, and shaved, I personally felt like a new person.

"Have you ever gone over the *aau* before?" the captain asked us.

"No. *Na fea ra?*" we asked.

"The main thing to remember is to keep calm and sit quietly; the boys know how to handle the boat, and they'll get you ashore safely. If the boat happens to overturn, make yourself as small as possible and let the waves carry you over the reef."

This was great news. We couldn't even float. This was the most mixed up kind of mixed emotion we had come to grips with so far. We were certainly sick and tired of the schooner, but what about that reef job ahead?

The small copra skow which had been lashed to the ship's side the entire voyage had now been let down into the water and had come alongside just below a short rope ladder. About one hundred and fifty copra sacks had been tossed down into the skow, then the baggage of those passengers going ashore. We were the last ones to descend into the skow. In a heavy sea this is no mean trick in itself as the schooner rocks high, leaving the skow far below. You are obliged to hold on until the ship rolls back; then you are on your own to drop on some well-chosen spot or trample over someone. It was quite embarrassing for Lilly Raye to descend, as she was dressed for getting on and off more conventional transportation and had not yet learned the native tricks of draping, tucking, and folding her frock. She landed with a resounding thud and sat down on the greasy copra sacks. We seemed to be overloaded for scaling a reef. We had previously read that to go ashore in this fashion we had to be picked up by the force of a wave and carried surfboard fashion over the reef. A heavy boat on a weak wave could be fatal.

"Aren't we a little overloaded?" I asked the boatswain.

He scanned the sea for a moment and answered, "I don't think so; the sea is heavy and the more weight we have the less likely we are to be overturned." That question increased the tension even more.

"I wish you would keep quiet. You ask some of the *scariest* questions," Lilly Raye said.

"If weight's what we need, let's go back and get the anchor." The joke was intended to break the tension. I had completely reversed my opinion about how to go over the reef.

We were now rowing toward a point supposed to be the pass but which looked little different than any other spot to us. The swells were very high, and the frail little skow was bobbing up and down like balsa. I kept trying to put on the brakes as we neared the reef, as it seemed we were getting a little too close to the crashing surf. We rowed dangerously close to the vicious reef and a cold sweat stood out on my forehead.

"Atira!" the boatswain called and the sailors stopped rowing. We had reached the crest of the last swell just before it crashed over the reef. The

Main street in Panou, Kaukura

boatswain was watching the rising swells some distance behind us.

We were staring ahead at the beautiful bushes of variously tinted coral flowers in a literal wilderness along the exposed reef. If the swell was particularly large we could see some fifteen or twenty feet of exposed reef below the surface. Then with a clap and a deafening roar the wave would charge under us and over the reef. We just rose on the crest and settled easily into the trough, for this was not the particular wave on which we were to skid ashore.

The boatswain was holding the rudder oar between his legs and putting his cigarettes and matches in his hat to keep them dry. He put a cigarette in his mouth and lit it. My first inclination was to explain to the boatswain that nicotine dulls the senses and that this was no time to dull anybody's senses, particularly the boatswain's, but before I could get the words out he yelled,

"A hoe, Haere i uta!" The four oarsmen strained on the oars and we moved even closer to the jagged reef. We were tipping forward at a dangerous angle and it seemed we were to be spilled head on into the grinding surf along the reef. We were looking full into a vicious wilderness of brittle and poisonous coral and within a split second would be smashed to bits with the force of the tremendous sea to cover us.

Just at that moment the swell jerked us high into the air, and now the bow of the skow was well above the reef; on our giant surfboard we skidded sideways over the barrier reef and scraped to a thrilling stop stern first about twenty-five feet behind the reef's edge in shallow and safe water.

My first attempt to rise found my knees uncooperative, and a nervous twitching gripped my stomach muscles.

The boatswain motioned for Lilly Raye and me to remain in the boat, but the others jumped immediately into the shallow lagoon and hurried ashore.

40

The sailors righted the skow, and with the aid of a secondary surf pushed us closer to the shore about a hundred feet away. The skow finally scraped to a full stop some few feet offshore, and two burly native sailors motioned for us to climb on their backs to be carried the remaining few feet to the white coral sand.

A native mission building,
in Papara

"Mauruuru roa," we said appreciatively, then turned to face a long grinning line of natives who had lined up to give us the handshake of welcome to Kaukura. First in line was the district president, Tuaora Fareata, followed by Rehia Bellais, governor of Kaukura; then came Rura, the local pastor, and Parara, his constant companion of about the same age and appearance. The local *chef-de-police,* Hiti Richmond, was also on hand. All of these men were priesthood members of the Reorganized Church. They were followed by a long line of inquisitive natives.

It was scorching, and we had been standing for some time in the hot sun. Finally the two venerable patriarchs of the island, Rura and Parara halted the procession and led us into the shade of a low unused cement lighthouse. Two giant coconuts were brought, and we were told to sit on them until the two-wheeled horse cart could be brought from the village about three quarters of a mile inland.

In the meantime the copra skow had made several trips over the reef and most of our heavy equipment which had been in the hold was now piled near our feet.

Soon an approaching gallop announced the arrival of our primitive transportation. Our heads were still swimming, and each time we stood up the land seemed to be swirling about. A wild-looking mare almost trampled over us as the young driver pulled the reins taut and brought the rickety cart to a skidding stop. He jumped quickly to the ground and ran up with his hand outstretched.

"Ia ora na orua," he said smilingly. He was a fine-looking young man, tall and energetic. He wasted no time loading our luggage and equipment.

"That's Saney Richmond," Tuaora said belatedly as we climbed aboard the two-wheeled cart. It was a jolting ride with a good portion of the population trailing along behind. Our voices vibrated a graph of the rough terrain covered by the jarring wheels. We were about to see what a real South Sea Island village was like.

Chapter 4

*Typical festivities with guests. Bishop
DeLapp and Apostle Hield are being
feted here*

An Island Feast

Evidently by prearrangement we passed by a long coconut-thatched building where about fifty fully clothed native children burst into a French greeting song. We had more or less envisioned a native welcome chant by half-naked savages, but we were born a century late.

Faimano was a typical native belle with large brown eyes, red hibiscus hair decoration, and dimpled cheeks. Her smile showed a full set of unnaturally white teeth. She had trained her children well for they sang in haunting harmony, even the tiny ones.

Somehow the village was not as we had expected. There was a predominance of European-style frame buildings with a very minimum of native thatch huts. The houses were clumped together along the main street with little respect for symmetry or style. The same pattern continued to the other two or three secondary streets even to the rim of shacks along the shore of the lagoon.

The stately breadfruit was everywhere in evidence and provided a welcome shade all along the route. We passed several unpainted two-story buildings which we were told were Chinese general stores. There were two frame church buildings at opposite ends of the village which seemed to blend into the rustic pattern of easy-going tropical activity. This was a fabled South Sea Island village spread out along narrow grass-covered and uneven streets.

We were taken to the home of the district president, Tuaora Fareata, who turned over his whole house to us and went to live with his adopted son just across the street. It was an old rambling house with an unusually large living room, kitchen and dining room combined, and an adjoining bathhouse behind. The full-sized front porch was to become our main living quarters and reception room.

Tuaora showed us over the house, pointed out the tub of fresh rain water for bathing and gestured toward the *fare iti,* which was one of the few constructed with a consideration for privacy, even if the door was only a colorful sarong dropcloth. We seemed to be the main attraction for the moment. The yard was full of natives squatting here and there and generally milling around to get a better vantage point just in case we decided to start opening our luggage and boxes.

Not being able to understand the Paumotuan dialect, the excited conversations sounded like jibberish at first. We sat on the porch for some time talking with the venerable patriarchs, Tuaora, Rura, and Parara who obligingly spoke Tahitian rather than their Paumotuan. Finally with a sharp command and a wave they sent the crowd away while we freshened up for the reception being planned in our honor.

At noon Hiti Richmond brought several hot casserole dishes which included chicken, noodles, roast pork, and potatoes.

"*Aue te maitai e!*" we exclaimed trying to show our appreciation. "To whom are we indebted besides yourself?"

"To Faimano my wife," he replied.

This was the first time we had connected a family relation. Hiti was the husband of the charming schoolteacher. They made a handsome couple indeed.

"Do you want to see how we prepare for a true *Ahi Maa* feast?" Hiti asked.

"*E! Nafea ra?* When will you begin?" We were more than eager to see a real earth oven feast prepared.

Hiti and Faimano Richmond

"Preparations have been going on all morning, but we will not be putting the food in the *Ahi Maa* until the sun is at this position." Hiti pointed to what I judged to be about three in the afternoon.

This was all the invitation we needed, and as soon as we had eaten we made our way to the area near the church where several groups of men and women were busily at work in the shade of the overhanging breadfruit trees. Many strange-looking dishes caught our fancy, and we began to ask questions about what they were and how they were prepared. We were first attracted to the men's department which seemed to deal mostly with the preparation of meat. We saw the clean white carcasses of several hogs hanging from the low branches of a *burao* tree. One group seemed to be dicing the meat and wrapping it in banana leaves. The suckling pigs, symbol of island hospitality, were to be left whole for baking. These were lined up on the ground on large clean leaves so prevalent in the tropics. Other meats in evidence, mainly fish, were being prepared by a group of laughing women who were sitting in a circle near by and seemingly enjoying their work.

We could identify the parrot fish, *paihere,* and tuna, but there were other kinds unknown to us. One was bloated up and bristled with spines resembling those of a porcupine. Clams, shrimp, and oysters in variety looked good enough to eat raw, but on the contrary it was the fish they were planning to eat raw while these delicacies were to be cooked in the earth oven.

The preparation of the raw fish dish was very interesting. The rawboned fish was cut up into small squares and cured in lime juice. The curing time depends upon the size of the chunks to be cured and the individual taste. The lime juice was then drained off, and the seared chunks of raw fish were rinsed and mixed with chopped raw onions, sliced tomatoes, and coconut milk. Not being a lover of this type of food I would simply describe the taste as a piece of vinegar-tanged, tender raw meat drowned in a thin coconut milk sauce. My teeth were willing, but my swallowing apparatus was weak. On the other hand, Lilly Raye ate it as though it was some palatable food.

Breadfruit was being prepared by still another group. First the rough skin resembling that of a hedge apple was scraped off with the sharp edge of a shell. The peeled breadfruit was washed, sliced, and the seed core removed. The breadfruit was then ready for the oven.

Banana *poi* was being made by a group of shy girls who were mashing skinned bananas in a wooden bowl with their bare hands. When they had worked this mixture to the desired consistency it was thickened by adding a heavy paste made of pulverized taro root. It was then sweetened to taste and a bean or two of vanilla added. This was stuffed into short length bamboo canes and was now ready for the *Ahi Maa* oven.

Other types of *poi* were similarly prepared by replacing the basic banana pulp with other pulps such as pumpkin, guava, papaya, or other palatable foods.

The *Ahi Maa* oven consists of several shallow gravelike pits lined with dry kindling wood. On the firewood is placed a row or two of dry coconut husks or other selected curing woods ostensibly to add flavor to the food. Carefully selected stones are then laid on the husks. (Some stones will explode when heated.)

The fire is lit, and when the stones settle and the fire has simmered to a white heat the food is carefully wrapped and laid on the stones. A layer or two of clean leaves serves as a cover and then dirt is shoveled over the entire oven leaving it completely covered in the ground. For several hours the food cooks in this manner before being opened.

Long tables covered with white cloths resembling bed sheets were arranged on the church lawn. It was evident that not half of the crowd could sit at tables.

The opening of the *Ahi Maa* oven was a ceremonial sight almost impossible to describe. The dirt was scraped off the oven and the layers of banana leaves peeled back removing all trace of dirt. Two young men wearing gloves were selected to lift out the steaming hot food. They laid out the food on a specially woven mat and immediately it was taken by an appointed person to a preparation table for dividing on the circular leaf dishes which had been woven for the occasion by a special committee.

50

The tables were soon laden with a variety of very delicious foods and our appetites which had been whetting all afternoon were soon to be gratified. We were seated for what seemed an eternity before the final touches were made and our good brother and pastor of the local group, Rura, arose to ask the blessing on the food.

Such descriptive adjectives as "terrific," "delicious," and "wonderful" were all too inadequate to actually convey the truth about the deliciousness of such a meal. The whole colorful evening was perfect, including the weather. The graceful moon shadows of the waving palms cast a spirit of romance as the shadows continuously waved a wand of magic over our feast table. The moon could not have been brighter. We could have read a book by its tropical brilliance.

From the porch of the church the young people were entertaining by singing the songs of the islands and strumming their improvised instruments in an intriguing manner. This was almost like a Hollywood balcony serenade.

The vivid pictures imprinted on our minds that night we hope will never be erased. Following the feast the usual number of fluent speeches were made and a gift service in our honor featured shells, *tifaifai* quilts, pandanus fans, a whale's tooth, a piece of flowered coral, canned fruit, and a small gift of money carefully folded and sealed in an envelope. We were then called upon to respond to the speeches, and after a short while the service was dismissed.

Chapter 5

A native village, Tahiti

Life on an Atoll

It must have been about five o'clock when we heard a persistent brushing sound outside. I looked out the window to see what was going on as it was yet hardly daybreak. A young girl about fourteen years old was sweeping up the large breadfruit leaves with a stiff coconut rib brush bound to a long handle with a strip of tin bearing the label "Salisbury corned beef."

"Certainly was a short night." I yawned.

"Good-a-morning!" The masculine voice startled me, as I had expected a reply from my wife. Lilly Raye sat bolt upright and drew the covers around her. "Who was that?" She blinked, shaking the sleep from her eyes.

"You sleep well last night?" Tuaora chuckled, realizing probably that his English was a little stiff.

I started outside in my pajamas to compliment Tuaora on his knowledge of English, but stopped short at the doorway as I discovered about a half dozen others of both sexes sitting around casually looking into our wide-open bedroom.

It was during moments like this that a handy knowledge of how to handle the *pareu* sarong would have been invaluable. We have seen natives dress without embarrassment in broad daylight by skillfully maneuvering the *pareu* cloth as a shield. This was not the time for experimentation.

We squeezed in behind a tall wardrobe and did a quick rumba shuffling into our clothes. The porch conversation was now in full swing and nobody seemed in the least embarrassed by our apparent disheveled appearance—except, of course, us.

The Main Attraction

A wash pan filled with fresh rain water drawn from the church cistern was sitting in the center of the porch. Evidently we had little choice, without being rude, but to wash up publicly. I broke the ice by forcing my extrovert personality to the fore. Actually I am naturally shy and shun public exhibitions of this kind, but my nature has always been to force myself to be equal to the occasion. I kept up my end of the conversation as I shaved, and finished with only the usual number of nicks. While I drew the attention of the crowd Lilly Raye had sponge bathed behind the wardrobe using our pitcher of drinking water. We came to appreciate that wardrobe more and more.

A small table was spread with a breakfast of cocoa, omelette, tinned butter, *pate,* jam, and a stack of Arnott's unleavened biscuits. This was being prepared in the same spotlight area as the shaving exhibition. Now a few others had arrived and taken up their positions along the railing as a sort of balcony cheering section to witness the entertainment, and we were to be the main attraction. We offered the blessing in English, but according to Lilly Raye (she peeked) we were the only ones who bowed our heads. This was not a sign of irreverence but of native curiosity, as few white visitors came to Kaukura for any length of stay. Actually we were enjoying every minute of our unique experience. After breakfast the dishes were whisked away and were evidently taken to a near-by hut to be washed.

"Ahu Repo anei, Edua?" Sister Tuarora Fareata was the Kaukura women's leader. I relayed her request to Lilly Raye who was at the time inside making up the bed. "Tuaora's wife wants to know if we have anything to wash."

We were not accustomed to such royal attention. We later learned that three separate food committees, each handling a different meal, had been assigned to us during our stay. Also a cleanup committee, water carrier, laundress, and personal guide —services gratis to us but for which an ordinary tourist would pay very dearly.

A two-wheeled horse-drawn cart was ready to take us sight-seeing. Remembering the rough ride from the wharf on yesterday, Lilly Raye declined the ride and asked to ride horseback instead. She had become proficient at this during her farm days at Erick, Oklahoma. I remembered the wild looking mare on yesterday and dampened that suggestion, particularly when we were told we would have to ride bareback and with a rope muzzle instead of reins.

We settled for bicycles and were soon pedaling along the narrow dusty road leading away from the quiet little village. The stately coconut trees were thick on both sides of the road from the ocean (*I tua*) to the lagoon (*I roto.*) It was easy to see that we were on a typical atoll. We pedaled leisurely along about an hour or so until the road finally dwindled to a narrow trail. Sometimes we were obliged to cross low areas which were actually under water. At one point the sandy texture of the soil slowed us until we had to dismount. Saney, who was our guide for the day, knew how to skirt these sand pits and was going on ahead. We called to him.

"Faafaaea rii tatou!" We had to have a breather and a chance to wipe off the sweat. He left his bicycle in the sparse shade and like a human fly began to walk up a near-by coconut tree without evident strain. He twisted off three coconuts and sent them spinning to the ground to keep them from breaking open and spilling the delicious nectar.

"This is strictly *opanihia*," he said, breathing heavily as he came up to us with an armload of coconuts. He took a long-bladed knife from his bicycle, chopped off the end of the nut and stabbed a hole in it so we could drink.

Precious Coconuts

"Will we be prosecuted?" I asked.

"*Aita.* This happens to be our own land, but we do have a local law which forbids drinking coconut water except in times of drought."

"What brought on that kind of legislation?" we asked.

Saney squatted down on a huge coconut and settled back to explain the whole affair which boils down to the fact that copra, which is the life line of the atoll, is spoiled if the nut is used for water before it is ripe.

We stayed in the area for some time. Finally Lilly Raye suggested, *"E ho'i paha tatou."* Evidently she felt that we had wandered far enough our first day on the island, so she requested we head back toward the village. Along the reef we noticed both men and women fishing. This seemed to be about the extent of the daytime activities as far as we could tell. Nothing seemed regular except the elementary school and church services.

Moonlight Stroll

Tonight was to be a full moon, and Hiti and Faimano had invited us to their home. They lived near the sea in a well-made neatly woven bamboo hut with a plaited pandanus roof. Modern type native furniture made a pleasant little home for the island *mutoi* chief and his *orometua vahine.* Faimano served a cool drink of fruit juice chilled in the only refrigerator on the island; this they had imported from Papeete. We visited with them for about an hour when several young people arrived with guitars and ukuleles. We were invited to go for a stroll with them along the beautiful sandy lagoon and through the bright moonlit streets of Kaukura. All the while we strolled we were serenaded with catchy syncopated rhythms.

The native language is never more beautiful than when it is expressed in song. Although we could not follow the *paumotuan* dialect, we caught on to the haunting melody and hummed along. Under the spell of this enchanted hour one could underscore the conclusions of Melville, Michener, and others that these are the islands of paradise. The color of that experience cannot be sufficiently transmitted literally.

Bananas, another important crop

Chapter 6

A pearl diver

Pearl Diving

The screaming hilarity at the little thatch theater on the fringe of the moonlit lagoon aroused our curiosity. We pressed into the already overcrowded house where a 16mm. Hollywood movie of pearl diving was showing.

It was hilarious even in the more serious parts, as accuracy had been sacrificed to the gods of the spectrum. The skin divers were doing the impossible. They kept up a flow of conversation to the very moment of the dive, then without the aid of diving weights they promptly plopped both feet on the ocean floor practically knee deep in the rare abalone shell.

The so-called pearl diver filled his flimsy basket to the brim on one trip and leisurely flippered his way to the surface, dragging the basket behind him. Promptly resuming the conversation he hardly showed a sign of heavy breathing. Both actors immediately began opening up the shell with their bare hands and scooping out great blobs of perfectly colored pearls, then cast the mother-of-pearl shell back into the lagoon with an over-the-shoulder throw.

The hilarity of this would not be appreciated by anyone more than by these professional aboriginal divers of the romantic South Seas.

The rarity of pearls is suggested by the fact that not one trace of a pearl that would even approach mediocrity was discovered in the Takapoto lagoon in 1957, despite the fact that over one hundred and fifty tons had been collected. Actually it is the mother-of-pearl shell the divers are seeking and not the precious by-product—the pearl.

"If you would like to see how real pearl diving is done," Tuao said after the show, "we can take you with us some morning." Brother Allen Breckenridge and I were eager to accept this invitation and suggested that Tuao pick a good day which would allow us to get pictures of the diving. It was a beautiful tropical morning several days later when Tuao brought us the news we had been waiting to hear.

"This is an ideal day for diving," he said. "The wind is *maitai roa*. The sun is *numera hoe*." Allen and I hurriedly gathered up our camera equipment and accessories including sunburn oil and followed Tuao to his sleek little *boti* lying quietly at anchor in the shallow green water fringing the coconut thatch village at Ngake.

Tuao is one of the finest spirited men we have in French Polynesia, and aside from the fact that he is a competent district president, he is also one of the most successful pearl divers among our people. We boarded the sloop and were soon under full sail, towing several motorless outriggers.

In a Blue Lagoon

The Takapoto lagoon is a small closed reef area of about eight miles expanse. Soon we were about a mile offshore and approaching a dark circular area about one hundred and fifty feet in diameter showing through the light blue water. This was one of the numberless such hidden coral stones in the lagoon which rear themselves from the lagoon floor until they nearly break surface in the form of a small islet.

When the lagoon is rough or the tide is out the whole surface of the coral head we were now approaching may be exposed momentarily to view as the swells rise and fall. The ideal areas for diving are near these stones, for the newly hatched abalone seek out these stones for lodgment where they will grow to maturity in three to six years. We cast anchor onto the shallow coral stone surface and made fast.

The initial act of preparation for the day's diving was for all who were connected in any way with the diving to bow their heads in a brief word of prayer as they sat reverently in their places in the canoe. This we found to be a universal practice among the natives of all faiths.

After the prayer the diver's assistant immediately measured the depth at which the diver would have to work by letting down the lead weight until it touched the lagoon floor, then counting the rope lengths as he pulled it up again. The circular rope basket was then lowered from the rear arm of the outrigger until it came to rest just short of the lagoon floor. This rope is secured firmly to the outrigger arm, for in this basket the shell taken from the sea is to be dumped. The weight makes a taut life line of this rope on which the diver depends as he pulls himself to the surface. The dangling basket also shows the diver the location of his canoe on the surface. At great depths the diver must never lose sight of his basket.

An Eerie Chant

During the preliminary preparations Tuao had changed from his regular clothing to a colorful *pareu* breechclout, and was now in the water beside the canoe. Every move he made seemed measured even to the cleaning of his diving goggles.

Perhaps the most interesting part of the whole procedure is the conditioning of the diver's lungs in preparation for the dive. He begins with a series of breathing exercises during which he may break out startlingly into an eerie chant or Western style yodel.

When he is ready to dive he lets the loop of his weight line slip over the outrigger arm and, standing on the fifteen-pound weight, descends slowly to the lagoon floor. Midway down he must feel a pressure adjustment in his ears or immediately ascend.

The assistant who remains in the outrigger watches the weight rope uncoil, and when it stops he knows the diver has reached bottom. He has strict instructions to hold onto the line at all times, for this is an emergency life line. If the diver runs into difficulty below and finds that he cannot surface by himself on the basket rope he swims quickly over to this auxiliary line, ties a quick knot around his wrist and jerks an SOS to his assistant who frantically pulls him up.

Great Depths

It is easy to see why the natives shun dark days for diving as the water should be clear as crystal especially at great depths. Murky water is a death hazard, since it would be easy to lose sight of both ropes.

Big ocean turtles

Unfortunately the most productive areas range from depths of 50 to 150 feet below the surface. The shells may be lying flat on the ocean floor but more frequently they are attached to the sides of the giant coral heads in whose dark recesses the vicious moray eel lurks. Against these dangers the diver has no protection, but he wears a protecting glove on his right hand to keep down infection from poisonous coral cuts.

The pearl shell is often embedded securely in the stone, and unless one is experienced in dislodging it precious energy needed to surface properly may be burned up. Some divers have been known to stay under water for periods up to three minutes, but a cautious diver will stay under only about one to two minutes. The average length of time Tuao spent under water was a minute and forty-five seconds, including both descent and ascent. This diving process is repeated about every ten minutes until the diver tires or gathers about twenty kilos of shell. This is an average day's take and will net the diver about fifteen or twenty dollars. The assistant is paid a percentage on each kilo.

Forming of a Pearl

If the diver feels any unusual signs of fatigue he will immediately stretch out on the canoe and rest. This gives the assistant time to draw up the basket of shell and dump it on the improvised plank table for cleaning.

He first chips off the barnacles and opens the shell by slipping a knife blade between the shell, severing the contraction muscle. In one motion a skillful operator can cut loose the meat, sound out the elusive pearl, and flip the meat back into the lagoon. This restocks the area by immediately releasing the imprisoned eggs. In lagoons with an open pass this is dangerous business, as man-eating fish are excited by fresh blood or fresh food of nearly any kind which is thrown haphazardly into the sea. In this case, the meat is collected in large pails until the diver has finished his day's work and come aboard. It is then dumped into the lagoon.

If the eggs are fertile, they will in time float to the surface to hatch in the sun. After hatching they must descend slowly through waters patrolled by hungry fish to find lodgment among the stones of the crustacean kingdom. Even if they survive these hazards and grow securely to the stones, they may be dislodged and devoured by the myriads of larger fish constantly driven by perpetual hunger to seek food among the stones of the lagoon.

If a grain of sand or other foreign object imbeds itself in the meat of the constantly opening abalone shell, the muscle secretes a substance which melts a portion of the sheen from the inside of the shell and forms a coating over the foreign object. The motion of the sea and the rhythm of the muscle opening and closing rolls the object into a small ball, and it builds up over the years into a beautiful ball of pearl.

If a diver's assistant discovers a pearl, the pearl belongs to the diver, although the assistant may be rewarded a share in proportion to the worth of the pearl.

Due to the great depths a pearl diver must work and the pressures he encounters, he must be very careful of his food intake. A glutton may find his entire meal disgorged under certain lagoon depth pressures. Even the best divers sometimes miscalculate, but a slight mistake in deep-sea diving can be costly.

Deep Sea Perils

The most pitiful result of extensive diving is the damage to brain tissue. Some of our most talented men have been reduced to simpletons by this strenuous occupation. Others have suffered major or minor strokes, and some have been disabled for life. There is also the ever-impending peril of sudden death from encounters with vicious undersea life.

The weather is the greatest single problem of the diving profession. Dark, cold, or windy days may discourage most divers, but oddly enough rain does not seem to bother them.

The return from the day's work may begin from noon to sunset, depending upon the mood of the diver and the incidence of pearl shell he has discovered. Once back at the rambling village, the assistant lays out the ropes to dry, takes care of the outrigger and generally cleans up the equipment. The diver takes the shell to the Chinese merchant where the pearl shell is weighed and recorded on his bill against which he charges his food and other purchases. His wife or hired cook generally has his evening meal waiting, and after a bath and a little food, he joins the rest of the clan in a repast of native delicacies.

The arrangement of houses in a typical diving village is haphazard. They are grouped by relatives or close friendships. Generally church members gather into a central area near the thatched assembly building. One reason for this is to facilitate their early morning and late evening devotions. One of their number is selected to ring the rising bell at 5:30 a.m. The regular church bell is not used. For this special devotional period a large bottle is struck with a piece of coral. This makes a very effective piercing sound at 5:30 a.m.

The natives within sound of the bell will arise and gather at the designated home or at the church. If they are off at some distance they gather at a home in that area for this short devotion.

We have a collection of experiences which are often thrilling encounters with sharks or narrow escapes from sudden death. Pearl diving is one of the most colorful occupations in the entire South Sea Islands in which both men and women participate. However, it seems to be a dying industry, not only from the dearth of pearl shell but from a lack of new divers. The younger generation seems to show little interest in the dangerous occupation.

Chapter 7

Spearfishing

Spearfishing

One beautiful evening we had a nine o'clock appointment to *turama* for fish. The incoming tide was just the right depth on the reef for one to be able to see the fish as they were forced up near the surface by the pounding surf.

We dressed in suitable clothes and were ready when Teiho Fauura came for us. He had a lighted gas lantern in case of torch trouble, four kerosene-soaked *turama* torches made of old burlap bags, two-, three-, and four-pronged spears, and an empty bag for carrying our catch. Teiho was a tall fine looking young man, the older brother of Abrahama, our youth leader at Papeete. These boys are the direct descendants of John Hawkins of church history fame. We made our way to the reef and waded single file to the choice area known best to Teiho. Lilly Raye followed immediately behind Teiho; I followed her; and several young natives trailed along behind us.

"*A rave orua i teie*." Teiho handed both Lilly Raye and me spears and continued, "If you see a fish *a patia ia'na!*"

Teiho handed the lantern to one of the other natives and ignited two of the *turama* torches. The place was literally ablaze and we could see very clearly into the crevices and crannies below the colorful surface. Teiho prodded into the darker areas and sent several fish across our path. At first we did not know what to expect and struck late or not at all, but generally the fish was impaled on a more accurate spear. We made several unsuccessful tries, but even if we didn't hit a fish we had fun denting the reef and watching the master fishermen at work.

Attacked by an Eel

The most exciting moment of the evening was the battle with an injured eel. The three-foot moray eel, a vicious serpent, was actually attacking us. *"Haapao Maitai!"* Teiho warned.

The eel skimmed along the surface of the water and with his gaping jaws set for the battle he headed directly toward us. We dodged and danced about, but before he could reach us with his razor sharp teeth, Teiho's spear had found its mark, going completely through him. The eel wound itself like a writhing cobra around the iron spear and mashed its teeth off as it bit into the iron.

The party was over so far as we softies were concerned. We could see that this was to be a survival of the fittest and we had more confidence in the opposition. Even small darting fish quickened the pulse beat after this frightening experience. But

*Natives carry on an easy life
at the edge of a lagoon*

we stuck it out for at least another hour and were rewarded by the sight of a marvelous variety of strange tropical fish, all sizes, shapes, and colors which were collected by our friends who seldom missed when they had time to aim with the spear.

Chapter 8

*Women's welcome song when President
Israel A. Smith and Bishop Mark
Siegfried visited the Islands*

Savage Rhythms

A plaintive chant broke the stillness of our tropical night.

"Ahay-hay-hay-hay . . . hay-hay-hay . . ."

It was a primitive chant issuing from the pinched throat of a male *perepere* singer. Generally there are two such singers required for the old-time singing. One begins the eerie cry at the very top of the human register and in rhythmic descent drops to the range of the second voice who carries the *perepere* to its climax—*Ahay-hay-hay-hay . . . hay-hay-hay.*

This is repeated without variation while the choir, huddled together and humped over looking straight toward the ground, sing in octaves varying from fifths to thirds in a chant of ancient words long since forgotten as to exact meaning.

The men especially seemed to rock their whole bodies back and forth in rhythm, and the very back row half hummed or groaned into cupped hands, giving the sound of wheezing bellows.

The chant was flawless in articulated sounds and seemed to pick up speed, if at all possible, as the chant proceeded. Every voice was constantly straining and the chanters were completely absorbed in their work. We could not catch many of the words, as they were of the *Parata* dialect spoken chiefly in the backward archipelago. Here were sounds we had never heard before.

This was a docile group of singers, but as the chant progressed and the tempo and force of the song increased they seemed to take on a savage appearance. One man leaped to his feet and started through a series of motions intended to whip up the speed of the chant. The faces of the chanters were seemingly warped into weird contortions. The women with tightly closed eyes raised their faces and nodded in rhythmic procession as they forced their voices to the very point of human endurance.

We had just witnessed the true native chant which was the only type of singing the early aborigines knew.

Almost without warning about eight young men came running out of nowhere with native drums made of various sized hollowed logs and with animal skins drawn tightly over two of the larger ones. They dropped into place near the singers and immediately two of the natives manipulating the smaller drums rattled out a preliminary drum beat impossible to describe.

Then the entire rhythm section burst forth with the most explosive, unusual, and captivating rhythms we have ever heard. With this background both men and women dancers applauded and tromped out a native stomp dance with arm, leg, and body movements portraying the chants we had just heard.

The dancers wore native grass skirts of colorful shreds of native bark dyed yellow with a root oil. Around their heads were garlands of woven fern greenery. Their bodies were soon glistening in the light of the dwindling fire in the center of the entertainment area.

Sacrifice and Violence

We could hardly realize that these were the docile, happy-go-lucky natives who had been milling around the village only a few hours ago. We were taken back to the ancient tribal festivities performed in earnest less than a century ago. Some of the chants spoke of human sacrifice, and many of the meanings were violent or immoral. We were glad to learn that few of our Latter Day Saint young people were among the entertainers.

"Does this go on all the time?" we asked one of the spectators on the fringe of the crowd.

"Chiefly during the Bastille day festivities," he answered. We had forgotten that this was the holiday season for all French Polynesia.

Church services had not been canceled despite the gaiety of the occasion, and so it was that we met as usual the following day which was Sunday.

Services on a lonely atoll do not vary much from the routine of customary procedure throughout the whole church. We have an early morning prayer service, followed by church school and eleven o'clock preaching.

True, the language used by the minister is strange to the untrained ear, but the message of the gospel is still the same. The natives preach of *Iesu Mesia,* show how baptism by immersion is necessary, how the laying on of hands confirms new members, heals the sick, ordains to the priesthood, as well as other familiar doctrines so often heard by Latter Day Saints.

"Himeneraa Faaao"

But one of the services not found anywhere else in all the world so far as the church is concerned is the nightlong song fest called *Himeneraa Faaao.* It was immediately at the close of the evening preaching service that we were all invited to go into the assembly building adjacent to the church to prepare for the *himeneraa.*

Tuaora was not only a popular minister with the young people but also the most capable man on the island, possessing a resonant ministerial voice. He and his two or three assistants sat behind a long table covered with a white linen cloth on the platform. The Three Standard Books of the church and an alarm clock were the only items on the table, with the exception of the invariable array of eye glasses in various stages of disrepair.

The beginning of the service was conventional with a song and a prayer, with the guitars remaining silent.

After the announcements the choir members noisily arranged themselves on two long backless benches and set out two benches just in front of them. At first only about two or three instrumental-

Stone court and native huts surrounding pyramid where human sacrifices were once made

ists occupied these front seats, but after about fifteen minutes of pleading from the stand, the instrumentalists filed in one by one and took up their places facing each other with their guitars and ukuleles which had been previously tuned outside. Evidently this was partly what had been holding up the show.

Ancient Styles

The first song was so different from what we had expected it was a little shocking. One high feminine voice broke the silence with a loud, boisterous sounding air, and after about three quarters of a phrase the whole group broke in with an intriguing harmony and rhythm. We could see some of the old ancient chant style in the manner in which this number was performed. The strumming guitars took the place of the humming bellows, and we thought we could detect in the rhythm of the guitar beat the drum rhythms of the savage dance ceremony we had previously witnessed.

The song was in pure Tahitian, and we caught the meaning of it which was a greeting song with our names mentioned in it. The song was carried on for several minutes repeating several times until the leader sent a nudge electric-shock-wise along both rows of instrumentalists. The end came startlingly abrupt as they sang with the full force of their lung capacity.

This type singing continued for about three solid hours with an occasional requested duet from Lilly Raye and me, which made a very weak competition indeed. Though evidently appreciated, judging from the response, it was probably endured as a necessary politeness to us.

We noticed that all of the songs seemed to take on a familiar pattern, and we were finally able to trace it to the fact that they were sung in the same key to accommodate the instrumentalists who were not able to modulate from key to key.

The songs dealt in general with religious topics including incidents of church history. We were not at all impressed with several songs dealing with the loves and intrigues of David and Solomon, although, ironically, these were the most lively of the entire lot, and before we grasped the true meanings had asked several times for a repetition of these songs.

It was now nearly midnight, and we were to witness a very welcome break in the monotony of the song fest.

"Coffee Break"

Tuaora had been interjecting some verses between the songs and brought out many good points of doctrine throughout the first half of the night. But now the books were laid aside and the guitars were stacked for a short coffee break.

The aroma of coffee had been drifting in from the open windows for the last hour or so. Now the aisles were filled with young ladies dressed in white with stacks of buttered bread on each arm. The long French loaves had been cut into thirds, sliced down the center and smeared with butter, then jammed together again. Each person was to get a third of a loaf, and we saw no refusals as they passed along the rows. The coffee had been boiling in two large five gallon gasoline drums and was now carried on the broad shoulders of two young men. They had a pole across their shoulders and the tin of coffee hung from the center on suspending wires. A selected matron dipped the steaming coffee from the large tin and filled the extended cups or bowls brought from home, cans, or other receptacles including rolled leaves which they improvised.

We could see that this was not something new to them. Everyone knew what to do. Two other assistants from the women's department followed along with sugar and coconut cream squeezed from fresh coconuts.

*The author explains a passage in
the Book of Mormon to a
young native*

Coconut Cream

We, however, were not to be subjected to such service. A special table was brought and spread before us with a clean white cloth covering. On it were a tin of Nestle's cocoa, a small pitcher of coconut cream, several large Arnott's biscuits, a tin of pears, and several kinds of small cake squares with whipped butter frosting.

It was a noisy but refreshing break. Everyone was enjoying himself, and the refreshments held out for at least two times around.

The second half of the night dragged on for us, but there was no apparent lack of interest on the part of the natives. One would ordinarily think a service such as this would automatically die after a few hours, but we were in for a surprise. Actually the tempo of the service increased. The men who had been more or less silent during the first half of the night now began to sing with gusto. At about four in the morning the pace quickened even more and the bursts of song became more vigorous, but the climax was reached at the crack of dawn when the first streak of red lighted the sky on the horizon of the lagoon seen from the wide windows of the assembly building. At this precise moment the roof seemed actually to vibrate with the sound waves set up by the tireless choir.

We shall never forget the experience of that night, for it was the first time in our lives we had witnessed a *Himeneraa Faaao*.

"Tero"

As had been predicted, the familiar sound of "Tero" announced the arrival of a ship. We would be leaving the island now to move on to another and possibly a repetition of these experiences. In less than an hour we were packed and waiting for the signal to board the schooner.

We walked to the seashore where just two weeks before we had made such a thrilling landing over the reef. It seemed that half of the populace was trailing along behind, chattering and laughing. As soon as we were gone they would all take a holiday and catch up on the sleep they had lost last night.

It took about fifteen minutes to walk leisurely from the village to the seashore. The area was alive with activity. The last copra bags were shoveled full and the women were sewing the sacks shut, using whalebone augers to draw strips of bark through the gunny sacks. The sacks were shouldered by strong copra carriers and dumped into the skow on which we also would ride out to sea to board the schooner which was cruising back and forth about half a mile out. The copra buyer had finished his work and was putting his papers away in his brief case.

Rura called for a song and the strain of *"E feia haere na te pahi"* was sung, followed by a fervent prayer for protection offered by Tuaora. This prayer impressed us, as we realized the imminent danger we faced going back across the reef in what seemed to us to be a very heavy sea.

Crumpled money was pressed into our hands as we shook hands once more with those who had followed us to the shore and took our places on the greasy copra sacks piled haphazardly on the skow which had been drawn as close as possible to shore to accommodate us.

Each small surf raised us a fraction of a foot as we inched our way toward the edge of the reef shelf to await the large wave that would lift us high enough to clear the dangerous reef.

Going out to sea from land is even more dangerous than coming ashore, as we were now bucking the sea rather than riding in on her power. It would be necessary to let the gigantic surf roll under us and as it receded to row out with it to the open sea. This sounds easy, but in a few moments we were jerked high by the pounding surf and because of the force of the wave we were turned sideways; the excited shouts of the natives heightened the tension as we realized we were again in danger.

Saney and others of the younger men on shore were running toward us through two or three feet of water in order to help out if we were overturned.

Dangerous Reef

We had been driven back by the force of the surf and as the natives rowed we did not seem to be making headway on the receding wave. We could not make it. We had reached a dangerous point on the reef, and if we scraped it at this time we were likely to be dumped into the sea. We struck the reef and as the wave left us momentarily high and dry the skow turned on its side nearly dumping us all out. Had not several of the sailors jumped out to hold it we would have been overturned.

Saney and his group had now arrived and actually hurtled into the boat, dropping right on top of us to add weight in anticipation of the next wave.

Unintelligible orders were being shouted by everyone except the missionaries who sat white as sheets,

their fingernails pressing into the sides of the skow. Here we were, sitting at a precarious angle on the very side of the slanting reef below sea level. The momentarily exposed jaws of poisonous coral glowed red as fire in the morning sun. Almost before we could realize it, a gigantic wave broke completely over us, drenching everyone on board but fortunately lifting us high and driving us sideways back beyond our former position. The extra weight had kept us from overturning.

Inches to Spare

Both Lilly Raye and I wanted to get off and go back, but no one seemed to be listening. The skow had been righted and pointed back into the sea.

Surely we were not going to try it again!

"A hoe! A hoe!" the boatswain shouted *"Haavitiviti! A hoe!"*

Leaning forward on the oars in co-ordinated unison every man strained backward to a prone position and continued this in a frenzied effort to ride this wave out far enough to clear the reef. Great beads of sweat stood out on our foreheads. With only inches to spare the skow again scraped bottom as we were sucked out to sea. We had finally cleared the reef.

It was not until we were well out to sea that the sweating oarsmen relaxed. It was only then we realized that our grip on the side of the boat had not relaxed. Jaw muscles were still taut and nervously twitching as we glanced back to see the little crowd of well-wishers waving to us. The older men who had realized our danger were wiping tears from their eyes.

We were leaving Kaukura, the first island visited in the dangerous archipelago.

Chapter 9

*John Mervin, businessman-minister,
and the author*

Marooned

Having successfully cleared the Kaukura reef we yet had one difficult operation, the transfer from the low rowboat to the lurching schooner cruising toward us about a quarter of a mile offshore.

The *Maoa'e* looked gigantic from our frail craft, and although her motors had been cut she stealthily overtook us with the appearance of an approaching monster. A sailor stood on the bow of our little skow holding a coiled rope which he prepared to throw up to the schooner to be made fast. Our oarsmen rowed us dangerously close to the path of the slithering ship.

Were we to be rammed and dumped this far offshore?

The bow of the approaching ship was now high above us, and just before we passed in front of the pitching vessel our towline was thrown up to the schooner's crew. We actually collided with the side of the schooner, but quickly pushed ourselves away to keep from being overturned as the heavy ship rolled toward us.

The towline was made fast to the schooner deck, and when our length of rope was taken up we were jerked mercilessly alongside. Our heads snapped back as we bumped along at the speed of the schooner. A rope net was dropped over the side and when a particularly large swell lifted us up we stepped high on the net leaving the skow to drop from under us. We clambered over the ship's rail and were greeted by our rotund and jovial captain friend, John Mervin.

"Ia ora na orua." It was like meeting a member of the family, for Brother Mervin was truly a wonderful person, a faithful minister, and a successful businessman.

"You've had a rough initiation in the Tuamotu," he consoled.

"I've just about decided that my next visit to Kaukura will come only after a pass is blasted through that treacherous reef." I could not have been more serious.

Tihoni, as he was affectionately known all over French Polynesia, had prepared our beds on deck under a tarpaulin canopy and advised us to lie down as he had noticed how white and quivering we were after such a chilling experience. I was already a little squeamish though we had not been on board over ten minutes. Tihoni left us momentarily to set the course for near-by Niau.

We lay down on our pallets and nestled down among the bulging copra sacks for a welcome rest. The mixture of diesel and copra fumes was so pungent it forbade sleep, but it added considerable flavor to our conversation.

"You and your big mouth!" Lilly Raye said.

90

Then she recounted a startlingly factual scene which ostensibly had taken place in America:

Joint Council: "Eddie Butterworth, will you go to Tahiti for about ten years?"

Eddie Butterworth (thinking from the teeth out): "Oh, yes, here am I, send me" (he learned that from a popular religious song).

Joint Council: "Does your wife approve?"

Eddie Butterworth: "Oh, yes. She loves that salty spray and the gentle balmy trade winds."

"Grrr! The salty spray turned out to be a cloudburst coming at me from every direction," Lilly Raye continued. "The balmy breezes have blown the bobby pins clear out of my hair."

I tried to console her by pointing out that our clothes were already beginning to dry out, but this was futile as she had already had experience with sea water and knew it would remain misty and damp until we could get to a source of fresh water. It was good to be able to laugh at ourselves, but there was no doubt about it, we had experienced a very rough time.

Niau was only about four hours away, but we had the inevitable motor trouble about halfway to our destination which delayed us a few hours more. We had almost convinced ourselves we could sleep when the stillness was broken by the sound of Tihoni's voice.

"Wanta see a *ma'o?*" We were on our feet instantly and hurried to the rail where Tihoni was leaning. He pointed out a twelve-foot shark which seemed to be circling our immobilized ship.

"Whenever the motors stop, the sharks generally gather to investigate," Tihoni explained. "Probably thinks we're a dead whale."

It was pleasanter here in the calmer waters and we felt a little more like conversing. We were glad to hear the news from Papeete, Brother and Sister J. Charles May were both well and had sent their best wishes to us. We told Tihoni of our fine visit to Kaukura and also shared some of our harrowing experiences.

Big Fish Story

It was a pleasure to be able to go from island to island by large schooner. Generally we were compelled to go by twelve-foot outboard motorboat over a very rough and treacherous sea.

Soon the motors were running again and we were underway at last for Niau. It was so pleasant now that we did not go back to lie down.

We made our way to the stern of the ship where we found a fish line with an unusually large hook. We untied the line and slowly let it out. We sat holding the line for about twenty minutes when all of a sudden the line snapped taut as though it had caught on the ocean floor. It was all we could do to hold the line until our excited shouts summoned assistance. A native sailor advised us to let out more line until the motors could be slowed down. It took several husky natives to pull in our catch.

Without committing the fisherman's sin we will simply say an ordinary gunny sack would hardly go

Typical motor boat used for interisland transport

over the fish's head. It was the largest fish we had ever caught, and it is not likely we shall ever catch another one as large. We were told it was of the tuna fish family. It was a far cry from our previous catch—a six-inch Missouri mud cat.

Beautiful Church

Niau is one of the smallest islands in the Tuamotu and shows up only as an insignificant dot on the map. It had been visible for some time, but we were so busy with the deep-sea fishing we had not noticed. Tihoni sent several of his most dependable sailors ashore on the first boat to test the pass and arrange for a shore crew to stand by to help us as we shot the reef again. We were all keyed up for another Kaukura reef experience, but fortunately we were in the lee of the island and the going ashore was routine. After the customary greeting and handshaking on the shore and a reluctant leavetaking of Brother Mervin, we were taken to the church, a large thick-walled structure built of gleaming white coral cement. It was a masterpiece of masonry supervised by a former missionary, Alvin Christenson, who we later learned had built many of our better churches in French Polynesia during his tenure of office in the 1930's.

Tepava a Teura, our native pastor, was our guide. We walked up into the three-sided balcony and around the premises of the enormous walled-in compound. Tepava was a pleasant, well-groomed man, straight and with a heavy mustache. We later learned he was also lieutenant governor of Niau. His associate pastor, Fareea, was also with us. Fareea was our bishop's agent and a very fine man, but he appeared too old to be very effective for an aggressive program. I learned, however, that he was one of the most trustworthy men on the island and one in whom the people had confidence to handle the church funds.

The Humming Storm Cloud

After the tour of the church premises we were taken to our home just across the street. The owner, Tiraha, was a woman of nearly seventy years with a copper-colored Indian wrinkled skin accentuated by a beautiful head of snowy white hair. Her features betrayed a native Chinese ancestry which accounted for her energy and frugality.

"Aue hoi e! Ia ora na orua." She kissed our hands and pulled us up onto the long wooden porch. All four rooms of the frame house were ours for the remainder of our stay on Niau. There was a clean bed in each of the four rooms, a dresser with a coal oil lamp, and a few straight-backed chairs. Mosquito netting hung from the ceiling and it was necessary to drop it each evening about five o'clock when the swarms of mosquitoes like a humming storm cloud struck the quiet village.

We dropped heavily into a chair on the porch and conversed with the natives who were by then teeming over the premises. Tiraha took Lilly Raye to show her the washhouse about ten or twelve feet beyond the back dining shed; it was joined to the main house by an overhead canopy of corrugated iron. She also pointed out the inevitable *fare iti,* and although it was provided with a door it was a laborious task to close it as it dragged on the ground. We spent the first day in getting acquainted with the people and the island generally, but we were soon into the routine work of checking the membership records. We had interviews with each member and arranged for six marriages to take place after ten days, the time allowed for pubic notice before a marriage can be allowed by law.

Wedding Procession

We had twenty-three public confessions and eleven baptisms. We held services each evening in the church, followed by a public song fest in the

A tropical paradise spot in Tahiti

assembly building. The first week passed rather quickly, and our work was arranged so we could leave by the first ship. We had not yet realized it, but the storms we had encountered from time to time were increasing in violence, and it finally became impossible for a ship to send a boat ashore at Niau. We waited another week and still another. We finally realized we were marooned on a tiny atoll in the South Pacific!

Our food had long since been depleted, but we were now learning to eat the native dishes which were surprisingly palatable.

Probably it was a good thing we were marooned, for it gave us a chance to see what the people were like after we were in their midst a few weeks. We had one banner day for weddings at which time six couples, followed by four attendants each, were married. As is the custom, they first marched to the governor's house to be married by him, then to the church. The church is but a half block away, and after the brief government ceremony we beheld a breath-taking sight. The entire bridal company arm in arm came down the road abreast; the governor was in the center with his tricolor badge of authority draped across his chest. Practically the whole village made up the multitude of inquisitive onlookers following along behind. In the foreground leading the entire procession was Tiraha, our good bronze-skinned hostess, mumbling an ancient wedding chant and gesturing from side to side.

We greeted the governor and shook hands with the bridal couples. After a briefing on how the church service was to be handled, Lilly Raye went inside to strike up the Lohengrin wedding march on her gleaming white accordion. It was the largest wedding ever to be held at Niau, and the largest one I had ever performed. Two days later we had two more weddings making a total of eight in all.

Ghosts and Superstitions

We were marooned on Niau for seven weeks and had one of the most unique experiences of our lives. We found that the natives were basically superstitious and believed in ghosts. Spirit mediums thrive on the ignorance of these people respecting the supernatural. One day while I was baptizing a young girl a giant dragonfly lit on my arm. I brushed it off unconcernedly and continued. Later, during a private seance, a Protestant spirit medium told the awestruck audience that the insect was the spirit of the dead mother of the young girl being baptized. This story was brought to our attention during the preliminaries to a preaching service when a dragonfly circled around our gas lantern hanging in the center of the building. An adult woman pointed out the insect to the girl and told her it was her mother's spirit. This called for an immediate change of sermon material to show the fallacy of that reasoning.

We were shocked to see the abysmal depth of darkness in respect to the teachings and philosophy of the church, but on the other hand the members all seemed to be loyal to the church. I had to shift gears in my methods and manner of preaching to these unfortunate people on this isolated and backward island. In a more educated society we are shielded from many of the crude sights including cases of mental disease which here met the public gaze daily. One who has had little experience with the effects of syphilitic spasms may actually believe the patient to be possessed with an evil spirit. A young Mormon missionary cracked up mentally at Tubuai because he was not aware of this.

The more primitive and less educated natives actually believe in supernatural powers in ancient stones and sacred bones. We find evidence even at Tahiti that some of our more enlightened natives place more confidence in the native medicine man than in the power of modern medication.

Back to Papeete

These things were brought noticeably to our attention at Niau because we were marooned there for so long. We also found that each afternoon, especially after a fresh rain, the natives gathered at a given spot for a sort of water sport. Because of the hilarity of the game and the regularity with which it took place we decided to investigate. We found that the young people, both male and female, were playing a water polo game in the nude. When they seemed unembarrassed by our approach we realized that we were in a very primitive society and again had to shift gears in our approach to their problems.

It was an unusual seven weeks indeed and as we look back on it, it was probably fortunate that we were marooned on this isolated island for so long.

A few days later the small copra schooner "Aito" arrived on its way back to Papeete. We were three days returning to Papeete and arrived at midnight, quite disheveled and spray soaked but wiser in the ways of life in the South Sea Islands.

Chapter 10

Walking on glowing hot stones

Walking in the Fire Pit

It was more or less on a dare that I decided to take off my shoes and enter into the strange *Umu Ti* ceremony at Papeete. Few people have a more tender, thin-skinned sole than I, but I had heard so much about this ritual I decided to investigate it.

The fire-walking site at Tipaerui was carefully selected by the natives several days in advance. It took nearly a week to prepare for the ceremony. Since some stones will explode when heated above a certain temperature, great care was taken in the selection of the stones necessary for the fire-walking ceremony.

A long trench not exceeding three feet in depth and eight feet across was prepared. It was lined with dry sticks and logs sufficient to burn for approximately twenty-four hours. The fire was so hot one could approach no closer than several yards of the *Umu Ti*.

The stones were glowing hot and now after twenty-four hours the fire was still licking up around the stones. Lilly Raye and I along with Alan and Gladys Tyree were pressed in among the throng of curious onlookers, trying to get a better look at the preliminary ritual. The sorcerer with a small bush of the sacred *Ti* leaf approached the trench, setting up a curious incantation supposedly a carry-over from the ancient Tahitian religion. The native priest struck the hot stones with the *Ti* leaves while muttering his weird chant in an almost forgotten language. He moved slowly out on the hot stones in his bare feet.

Absolute silence reigned during this very impressive ritual and the throng stood in rapt attention. After the priest and his troop reached the end of the pit he turned and invited those who wanted to go across to follow as he had done but issued a solemn warning not to look backward under penalty of the hot stones biting into their flesh. Many of the curious including some children bounded across the stones. This was a golden opportunity that might never present itself again, so I decided to go across.

"Will you accompany me across the *Umu Ti?*" I asked Brother Tyree.

"Just leave me out," he said. "I'll stay on the sidelines and record your historic trip on film."

"Hold your flash," I said, "until I get to the center of the pit, then I'll turn around for a real 'Ipana' pose."

This was a direct affront to the authority of the sorcerer, but this was an experiment.

I stepped down onto the stones and started across the *Umu Ti*. The heat was intense around the face, and the fire was still licking up around the stones. Most tenderfeet like myself would hesitate to move out too far under these conditions onto the hot stones, but I had already determined to go and

102

could not stop now. The undersides of the stones glowed alternately white and red, but the top surface, though warm enough to discourage standing still, was far from biting hot.

When I reached the halfway point I turned around for a flash shot by Brother Tyree. There was no additional sensation except a mental pressure which tried to suggest that my feet were actually hot, but I was able to subdue this mental suggestion. After the flash shot was made I continued across the pit and then returned, going in the opposite direction without the stones biting into my flesh as was prophesied by the native priest.

"What do you think of the *Umu Ti* ceremony?" Brother Tyree asked later.

I told him I thought the secret of the ritual is in the selection of stones which are not good conductors of heat.

The stones were visibly hot on the bottom, but the full intensity of heat did not reach the surface of the stones. The terrific heat from below the stones struck me forcibly in the face when I walked across the fire pit but I was convinced that it was only the rising heat from below the stones accentuated by the pressing throng which tended to concentrate the heat in the center area.

It is possible that without a strict mental control one could easily give way to the power of suggestion and find his feet actually burning.

I found no supernatural power connected with the *Umu Ti* ceremony.

Chapter 11

King Pomare's tomb

Horahitu, Tahitian Royalty

He was the kind of man who would stand out in a crowd.

He was tall, raw-boned, with American Indian features. He held the dignified bearing of a man of good parentage. His outstretched hand seemed to swallow ours in a vigorous handshake of welcome to Tahiti.

This was the beginning of a long and profitable friendship with Horahitu, our native missionary. Horahitu accompanied us on many of our missionary trips to the outer islands and proved to be a wonderful companion and capable minister. It was during these extended missionary tours that we became intimately acquainted.

"Have you kept a diary of your life?"

Horahitu smiled at my question and shook his head. "No, but most of the important happenings in my life are still pretty vivid."

"Just what is your relationship to the Royal Pomare family?" I inquired.

"Do you see this *raau turutootoo?*" He held up a beautifully carved walking stick. "It belonged to Pomare V, the last king of Tahiti. It was given to my father, Teriinohorai Tauhitia Tati, who was a high chief and close relative of the king. He sat

105

regularly in council during the final days of the native government. It is a long time ago, but I still recall it was my father who helped prepare the king's body for burial.

"The public had not yet been notified of his passing. There was a great stir in the palace and I remember how frightened I was when the French honor guard arrived. I can recall walking along with the sad family procession just behind the hearse which bore the king's body to the tomb at Arue.

"One week after the burial, all the chiefs under the king and the close relatives (my father qualified on both counts) were summoned to the Pomare palace for an important meeting. The outcome of this meeting was a decision to secede to France. When the appointed day arrived, the large palace yard at Papeete was jammed with people. I was on the palace porch with my father. The Tahitian flag was flying high in the breeze in the center of the courtyard. French soldiers in full dress stood erect near the base of the flagpole.

Memorable Ceremony

"The representatives of France arrived, and all of the officials took their places near the Tahitian flag where Pomare's eldest living son, Prince Hinoi, represented Tahiti in the secession ceremonies. The captain of the French honor guard raised his signal sword and when it was dropped, the cannons sounded a salute.

"I did not fully understand the import of the occasion at the time, but I remember well that there

106

*The patriarch, Horahitu, in the company of
Bishop DeLapp, Apostle Hield, and others*

was a tug of terror on my heart as I watched the
solemn ceremonies. The French representative
spoke briefly about the previous agreement between
the two governments, that upon the death of the
king the French were to assume control of Tahiti.
He asked if Tahiti had a statement to make.

"Nothing was said and the quietness seemed
very intense, broken finally by my father who slowly
lowered the Tahitian flag from her proud pinnacle,
folded it, kissed it, and handed it to Prince Hinoi.
The prince handed it to the French representative
without kissing it or without any show of emotion
of any kind.

"A French flag was produced and my father raised
it to the top of the pole where significantly it hung
limp, for there was even a hush of the elements at

that precise moment. The reign of Tahitian kings had ended, and the rule of the French had begun.

"Generous gifts of money were handed to the prince, to Marau, the late king's wife, and to my father. All of the children of the royal family received monthly checks during their lifetime. Since the death of my father we have not received dividends from the government."

"You have not mentioned your mother, Horahitu." (I noticed before that the women do not seem to rate very high in the Polynesian society.)

"My mother's name was Raita Timo Viriamu Smith."

"With a good name like that," I broke in, "no wonder you found the church." I was only joking, but he hastened to explain how he became connected with the church.

Conversion to the Church

"I was a convert to the church. Formerly a Protestant, I became attracted to the church by the good life of my Latter Day Saint companion and the sincere ministry of that Paumotuan linguist, Hinman Savage. One of the high points of my experience in the church was my trip to the 1930 Centennial Conference with Brother and Sister Joseph Yager, at which time I was sent out under General Conference appointment as a missionary."

"You are too modest, Horahitu," I said. "You have not mentioned your many successes in the missionary field."

"I have had little success," he said and smiled. "The real credit for the success of the work in this part of the vineyard must go to such devoted ministers as T. W. Smith, Paul Hanson, Joseph Burton, and their families who followed them into this field, not to forget, of course, the more recent missionaries like Robert Brown and R. J. Farthing. There were others who made fine contributions, but their names do not come to mind right now. My life has been enriched by the association of all these brethren."

While Horahitu was in the reminiscing mood I asked another question: "Do you remember the ship *Te Evanelia?*"

"I remember it very well," Horahitu said. "They should never have gone into commercial shipping with our little missionary boat."

Tomb of the queen,
wife of King Pomare

We were inclined to agree with him, but we were not aware of all the circumstances which made this necessary.

"I was very thrilled to see the slide pictures of Brother and Sister Case which you showed some time ago on the screen and to know that they were still living." Horahitu's eyes shone as we discussed these aged and beloved missionaries who labored in this field many years ago.

"Another fine man," Horahitu continued, "was Brother Charles Lake who is buried in the *rahui* at Amanu."

"It seems a shame," I said, "that we have not brought his body to Papeete for burial at Paurani. We could build a crypt on the site of Sister Ellis' grave and provide for several burials in a very over-crowded cemetery."

"The Amanu folk are very proud of that grave site," he said. "They have taken good care of it over the years."

I could see that Horahitu did not agree that the body should be removed. "If ever we decide to bring his remains to Papeete," I consoled, "we shall leave an appropriate marker at Amanu."

Clyde Ellis

I was surprised that Horahitu had not mentioned Brother Clyde Ellis, as they were always very close. I drew him out on this subject.

"I have heard that Brother Ellis knew the Tahitian language pretty well. Is that true?"

110

President Israel A. Smith,
leaving Tahiti

"Not only was he a master of the language," he said, "but he knew the peculiar cultural patterns of my people better than we knew them ourselves." Horahitu's eyes moistened as he continued: "He was a rare minister indeed. His wife Clara and my first wife both died in the flu scourge of 1918. I could not have borne my burden so easily had it not been for the strength of character shown by Taraita during that trying time." The conversation quickened at this point and it was easy to see that Horahitu loved this good apostle very much.

"Can you think of any other high points in your ministry, Horahitu?" I asked.

"The Taravao Conference of 1951 presided over by President Israel A. Smith was a high point in my life.

A Spell of Leprosy

"I am inclined to agree with my people who believe that President Smith is a true prophet of God

111

and a man of unusual power. We felt this the moment of his arrival at Papeete and the stirring of the elements as he set foot on the wharf confirmed our feelings. Do you remember what happened that day, *Edua?"*

"Yes, Horahitu," I replied, "it did seem strange that the wind should blow so furiously, in fact, so hard that several tin sheets of roofing were torn from the near-by copra sheds, just as his plane arrived, then to subside so noticeably just as he stepped ashore from the launch."

Horahitu eagerly continued, "But his visit to the tomb of my ancestor, King Pomare V, is the most miraculous happening of all. How many representatives of royalty from all over the world have visited the tomb over the intervening years since the sealing of the shrine, yet only President Smith has actually entered the tomb to honor the last King of Tahiti."

"Brother Breckenridge and I were with President Smith that day," I interjected. "We had explained to him that there had been a strong belief among the natives that a spell of leprosy has long hung over the tomb, and that anyone who touched the tomb would be smitten with the disease. President Smith only smiled at this and walked up to the door of the tomb. He merely seemed to touch the door with his index finger, yet it fell suddenly to the floor. He casually entered the tomb and the rotten floor crunched under his feet as he walked to the dusty casket containing the body of the King. He placed his hand on the bier and stood there silently for a minute or so. He examined the pictures yellowed with age which hung around the walls and finally came outside. We helped him replace the door while a small group of wide-eyed onlookers watched at a safe distance. I presume they expected President Smith to emerge covered with leprosy."

"No, *Edua,*" Horahitu hastened to explain. "It is the belief of the people here that the spell of leprosy was broken when the prophet entered the tomb. This was confirmed a few days later when we visited the leper colony with President Smith."

A Powerful Spirit

"It was a very singular experience indeed," I added. "President Smith was not normally an emotional man, but he was completely overcome at that time and actually could not speak. It was a little embarrassing to me, for I was to translate for him, but after the first word or two he paused for a full minute or so with the tears streaming down his face. We waited still longer, but he evidently could not continue at that time. In order to relieve the pressure on President Smith, I began to speak to the lepers. There was a powerful spirit present. I told the lepers that President Smith was completely overcome with compassion for them because they were confined to this lonely exile from society.

"The five members of the church, who had been standing at the railing eagerly waiting to hear the

Church members in a leper colony

prophet speak, also seemed overcome to the point of exhaustion. The Lord may have used this very moment to touch the earth with his light of knowledge and may have quickened the intellect of those dedicated scientists who have been laboriously seeking to find a substitute for the foul-tasting chaulmoogra oil which, though not a cure, was often distinctly beneficial."

A Miracle

"There is no doubt about it," Horahitu said emphatically. "As long as I can remember we have had members of the church confined to the colony. Where are they now?" This was a good question. Brother Tahua Richmond, who had been an inmate

114

of the colony for over thirty years, was the first to respond to treatment and was actually given permission to leave the colony. He chose, however, to remain until his daughter Ema could leave with him. Unfortunately he succumbed to another malady before this occurred. Ema had been in the colony for approximately fifteen years, but today she is free and living a normal life outside the colony. Munanui, whose rough fingerless hand we shook before leaving Tahiti, is now working his copra farm in the outer fringe of the Tuamotuan Archipelago. The two young Paumotuan lads who were more or less recently committed to the colony are now back with their families.

"Is not this a miracle, *Edua?*" Horahitu asked.

"Yes, Horahitu, we are compelled to believe that a miracle has been performed. It was only a few weeks after President Smith left Tahiti that I saw Sister Ema Richmond's eyebrows begin to grow back again. I shall never forget the few words President Smith was able to utter at the colony that day. He said, in response to a gift of a highly polished wooden crab given to him by the lepers, 'I shall place this on my desk at the Auditorium and each time I look upon it I shall utter a prayer for you.' I sincerely believe his prayers for these unfortunate people ascended to the throne of grace and that a miracle has been performed."

Chapter 12

A quiet lagoon

Through the Jungle

Seventy-two torturous hours after leaving Papeete, our cargo-laden schooner chugged into a wide rock-strewn pass. We dropped anchor in a beautiful lagoon about one hundred yards from a long narrow wharf extending its hand of welcome toward us.

A steady gale swept down upon us from the low mountain crags and whistled an eerie tune through the ship's rigging. The island of Raivavae is one of the Austral Islands, the southernmost cluster in French Polynesia. In comparison to its size, the mountains of Raivavae outsnaggle-tooth the mother island, Tahiti. Eight hundred people are sprinkled sporadically over the island in four quaint little villages, connected only by bridle paths a kilometer or so in length which spiderweb over the low hills.

This was the first stop toward our destination, Tubuai. Our statistical records showed but one member living on Raivavae, so with the feeling of a shepherd leaving his ninety and nine to find the one lost sheep, I set out to begin the search. The whale-boat was loaded with island staples and ready to go ashore. We jumped down on the bags of flour, sugar, and rice and were soon rowed to land.

As is usually the case upon the arrival of the inter-island schooners, the dingy Chinese shops come alive with activity. I sat down heavily, almost unnoticed, on a sack of coffee beans near the door of the shop and watched the excitement. It had been over a month since a ship had visited here, and we had expected a mad scramble for food for the half-starved and naked children so much in evidence all about us.

The scene turned unexpectedly into a stoic pageant of sullen-faced mothers parroting a monotonous request for tobacco. The abject ignorance was even more pitiful in the cases where hungry children were clinging expectantly to their mothers' skirts. It was plain to see that the gospel of Jesus Christ had not taken root here. A wave of compassion came over me, and I wanted to shout the tidings of salvation as revealed to us in the fullness of the gospel. But the island already boasted of Christianity; in fact 90 per cent of the people were baptized members of a popular denomination.

Little circles of mixed youth squatted here and there participating in some sort of game of chance played with rows of stones in rude squares marked on the ground. Their boisterous laughter and gestures indicated a very unwholesome atmosphere.

"Ia ora na, popaa." A middle-aged man was the first person to draw me into conversation, but it was unflattering to learn that all he wanted was someone to tie his necktie. He was the governor of the island and was getting ready to go to church, for this was Sunday morning and our schooner had brought a visiting minister. The church bell tolled

*An arrangement of native handwork.
The flower is called "Flower of
Tahiti" (Tiare Tahiti)*

out the invitation, or warning as the case might be, and a large number of people made their way to the church which was surrounded by a low cement wall.

There was a predominance of white wearing apparel. The women wore homemade hats of woven pandanus fronds but were invariably barefooted. The men wore semiwhite coats frayed at the collar and sleeves, with blue denim or other darker material below the waist. Those who did not go into the small coral-cement church took up positions along the low sea wall which surrounded the property.

I overheard the local governor, whose tie I had tied earlier, attempting to bribe the supercargo for a case or two of intoxicants, for the Christmas season was approaching.

Off on a Jungle Trek

"Are you acquainted on this island, *Edua?*" I had not noticed Taroa approaching. Taroa Maitepua was an inactive member of our church who was a fellow passenger on our schooner from Tahiti on his way home to Tubuai.

"No, Taroa, but I'm looking for an elderly woman whose name appears on the church records. We have not heard from her for years."

Taroa volunteered to help with the search and was soon able to find someone who recognized the name of the person we were seeking.

"She lives on the other side of the *Mou'a*," Taroa said. Unfortunately I had on Chinese *savottes* unsuited for mountain climbing, which soon wore blisters on both feet. It was finally necessary to sling the sandals over my shoulder and proceed barefoot.

Taroa was a gaunt Ichabod Crane sort of fellow in appearance but a very pleasant and considerate traveling companion. Our singular trail ended frequently in the very dooryard of native thatch huts. It was necessary to walk around these dwellings and test several of the paths plunging on into the jungle to find the main thoroughfare. We soon discovered that the most obvious paths did not necessarily mean we were on the right track.

Low branches laden with coffee beans in various stages of ripening had to be ducked. Banana palms flicked us from both sides. Oranges, mangoes, breadfruit, and pineapple were in superabundance. Generally a thick patch of taro heralded the near approach of an inhabited area. My feet were burning, and the damp clay soil in the dense shade of the overgrowth felt good as we plodded along. We met few pedestrians on the trail, but those we did meet were very startled to find a white man pushing along in the jungle and even more startled to have us speak to them in a dialect of their own tongue. They gave us a wide berth and stood silently some few feet in the thicket to peer at us as long as they could through the dense foliage of this fantastic world.

Animals darting across the path consisted mostly of mangy dogs and skinny cats and pigs. I saw a dog roasting on an improvised rotisserie in one of the native enclosures we had passed through earlier, and I was certain that roasted dog was served us when we accepted an invitation to dine in one of the huts during the trip.

Initials on a Burao Tree

Tame goats were generally tied with ropes of twisted vines to keep them from wandering into unfriendly camps. Broods of scavenger chickens took their startled flight every few hundred feet.

We had been climbing for nearly an hour, including periodic rest stops, and had finally reached a clearing which showed the rest of the ascending path a few hundred feet ahead. It led over a saddle ridge between two high peaks. It was a laborious effort to reach the summit, but a feeling of accomplishment was an awarding feature not to exceed the refreshing rest under a broadleaf tropical tree. This was an often-used rendezvous from all appearances, and we added our crude initials to the others in the burao tree near by. From this breathtaking vantage point one could see both sides of the island and far out to sea in all directions. Our little schooner, bobbing gently at anchor in the crescent lagoon far below, to all appearances was but a toy. The clear outline of the reef was colorfully plain, and the channel from the pass to our anchorage spot seemed frighteningly narrow. We did not delay the descent, for Taroa pointed out a refreshing stream gushing down the opposite side. The descent was little different from the ascent except that startled bathers in various stages of undress were forced to make some quick decisions.

A Jungle Meal

The huts became more numerous near the bottom of the trail, and in one of them we stopped for some refreshments which turned out to be a veritable feast. The table was set with all manner of delicacy for the accustomed palate. Tahitian poi is one native dish of which I am particularly fond, so it was with unusual anticipation that I stripped down the banana-leaf covering from my individual portion of Austral Island *popoi*. The experience was disappointing, for it was nothing like the Tahitian

A typical jungle home

poi. The consistency and flavor were that of sour dough approaching the inedible stage. It was a palatable delicacy, however, for Taroa, who, along with several others, stabbed his index finger into the main *popoi* bowl in the center of the table and wound a good-sized mouthful on his finger and plunged it regularly into his big mouth.

Watching Taroa, I soon detected my mistake. I was chewing the stuff, while he let it slide down without a tooth touching it. I did not offer to finish my serving, nor did I dare try the eight-inch flapjacks piled near by which seemed to have been pressed with a hot flatiron. We were able to satisfy our hunger, however, for there was an abundance of boiled fish and taro root.

It was refreshing to find such genial hosts and such genuine hospitality in this strange jungle. We thanked our friends and continued our trip, for the home of our good sister was still a kilometer or so away. The going was much easier now that we were at sea level again. We walked along the shore, and the salt water licking at our feet was very soothing indeed. But even on the beach a tenderfoot has to pick his way carefully, for the large ironwood trees which fringe the shore have shed their coarse burrs all over the shifting sands. Through a clearing we saw a neat little hut with an adjoining cookshack under a plaited lean-to of pandanus fronds. This was the description of the house we were seeking. Taroa soon motioned for me to approach, and I could tell by the look on his face that we had finally found the house we were looking for.

Worship in a Jungle Hut

"Haere mai, Edua." Our aged sister kissed my hand and leveled a stool in the sandy floor of the open cookhouse. I sat down and immediately began to massage my aching feet. With trouser legs rolled almost to the knees and both feet in a pan of cool water, I carried my share of a three-way conversation for nearly three quarters of an hour. The conversation turned to food, and we were again invited to eat.

Later, several neighbors and friends were invited over for a church service. We shall never forget that cottage meeting in the jungles of Raivavae. The

124

revival of the faith of our good sister who had lost contact with the church for over thirty years was strengthened further by the request of a young sister who before the meeting was over expressed her joy of having found the Church of Jesus Christ, which is called in the Tahitian language TE EKARESIA A IESU MESIA I FAAAPIHIA NO TE FEIA MOʻA I TE MAU MAHANA HOPEA NEI.

Chapter 13

A museum piece: a stone idol—on Tahiti

Antiquity and Superstition

In appearance, Tubuai is not unlike Raivavae except on a larger scale and with an edge of beauty unexcelled anywhere in French Polynesia.

It is an overnight cruise between these two islands. The first sight of Tubuai in the early morning hours stirred exciting memories of church history. It was here in April, 1844, that the good ship "Timoleon" dropped anchor and the first Latter Day Saint missionaries set foot in Polynesia. It was on Tubuai that the first convert to the church was made by Addison Pratt. The church's first sacrament of the Lord's Supper in French Polynesia was served here, and many other firsts transpired on this historic island.

We had a feeling of brushing with antiquity as we stepped ashore. We were met by our native carpenter-missionary, Taiura Piehi, and a committee of local elders who took us to a recently built mission house at Mataura where we could freshen up.

I was told that the best time to take photographs of the church properties (a hobby of mine) was in the early morning hours, so we set out immediately for the most distant congregation called "Mahu." It was a tiring trip by bicycle, especially since we were so laden with equipment draped over our shoulders and over the handle bars. At Mahu we saw the monument erected on the sight of the first church building in Polynesia, and the stream where the first converts were said to have been baptized.

It was an indescribable thrill to walk over this sacred ground. The church at Mahu was in disrepair and we were told that the shift of population to Taahuaia and Mataura had made it necessay to consider disorganization of this branch. On the basis of its roots in the history of the mission we delayed making a decision on the matter.

"Do you see these *ofai* here in the church yard?" Taiura pointed to several stones lying half buried in the earth.

"Of what significance are they?" I asked.

"The elders here refuse to move them. They say they are tabu," Taiura continued.

I had run into evidences of superstition all over the mission and it was not always the ignorant class who believed in the powers of tabus, ghosts, and witchcraft. Many of our sermons and class periods were devoted to discussions of these topics in an effort to educate the people away from these old superstitions. It is hard to tell whether we are making headway.

Forms of Magic

On one of the Austral Islands we saw the inhabitants line the beach with dried coconut fronds and ignite them just as we landed, making it necessary for us to jump through a sheet of flame and smoke to get ashore. I learned that this has been going on for years and must certainly stem from some ancient superstition. Various forms of magic still persist in Polynesia which included porpoise calling, fish magic, seances, medicine magic, ghosts, fire-walking, and weird incantations and ecstasy chants. It should not be strange that few of these are successful when tried in the presence of the missionaries. I have seen natives doctor a misery in the right foot by applying an herb concoction to the left foot. At Hikueru in 1946 I was called out in the middle of the night to dispel a houseful of demons which were said to be clearly visible.

One persistent superstition which plagued us during our stay in Polynesia was that stormy seas were caused by the presence of missionaries on board ship. My shipwreck on the island of Rairoa in 1953 seemed to lend authority to this conclusion. In spite of all our efforts to disprove this superstition, it has stubbornly persisted. It may be a carry-over from the biblical story of Jonah, or it may have even deeper roots in native antiquity, but whatever the source it seemed to be an unshakable part of Polynesian superstition.

Just before leaving Tubuai I overheard a casual conversation between two Protestant natives who were blaming me and their own minister, who had arrived on the same ship, for the rough seas we had encountered on our trip. It seemed useless to engage in a lengthy defense, so we passed it off, but it was not to end there. The last day on Tubuai was a full day of sermons and at least three full-fledged feasts were held at the three congregations of our church on this beautiful island.

Impending Storm

The schooner, which had been lying at anchor in the lagoon, had long since passed into the open sea, for the captain feared the impending storm might hurl the ship against the sides of the narrow pass, and with darkness coming on this could be disastrous. We shall ever be indebted to the captain and crew who gave us all the time we needed to finish our work on Tubuai before having to leave.

At nine o'clock in the evening I boarded the rowboat with several other passengers who had remained ashore a few extra hours, taking advantage of my good fortune. We were rowed approximately a mile out to sea, passing uneventfully over the reef in almost total darkness.

We signaled the schooner with our six-cell flashlight and tried to get him to come closer to us. But the captain refused to sail toward the reef at this hour and in this tempestuous sea. We rowed for approximately fifteen minutes before reaching the bobbing schooner.

We boarded with considerable difficulty, clinging desperately to the ship which was rocking precariously. We made our way below to the captain's room where he had been confined with flu since we left Tahiti over a week before.

"I'm sorry I've held you up so long, Captain, but I sincerely thank you for allowing me to finish my work ashore."

"That's all right, *Edua*," the captain replied. "We can't leave anyway in this weather."

A Lurching Ship

Even though we were securely anchored to a submerged coral head we were thrashing about precariously. I flipped on the captain's radio and began administering antibiotics to him. These had kept him going since he left Tahiti, but I had not seen him for a couple of days and he had suffered a relapse. We heard a weather report which indicated that the wind in the Austral seas was rising and we were firsthand witnesses of the fact.

We were all having difficulty keeping our balance as the ship lurched about. It was the captain's plan to remain here at anchor until morning with the hope that the sea would subside in the meantime.

But suddenly a huge swell snapped the eight-inch anchor chain with a resounding jolt and our ship was swept toward the reef. The sick captain went flying from his bunk as he felt the ship break from its moorings. Luckily the motors were running, and a frantic series of bell signals and excited vocal orders soon brought the ship under control.

Everyone was now on deck and in the dim lights of the schooner my eyes fell on the two men who had earlier in the day blamed the rough sea on their minister and me. Evidently they didn't realize I was leaving on this ship or they might

Punishment in stocks

not have risked going. To top it all off, I then
recognized the sailor at the tiller as the one who
held the wheel when we were wrecked on the
reef at Rairoa, barely escaping with our lives. The
captain gave orders to get quickly away from land
but warned that even this was dangerous as we
were overloaded with copra and the seas were too
rough to navigate safely.

I helped the aged captain back to his cabin and
sat down beside him to translate health instructions from our Mercks manual.

If we should lose the captain we had no one
on board who could steer us safely back to Papeete.
The first mate was a rough native man of powerful build, but he was not qualified to travel these
dangerous seas in the South Pacific. He burst into
the cabin and asked the captain for orders.

"Shall we head for Tahiti?" he shouted. The captain raised himself laboriously on one elbow and holding his head with the other hand he wheezed, "Use your own judgment. I'm too sick to . . ." He cut his words short as he glanced at me and dropped back on his sweat-sogged and yellow-stained pillow.

"What's the compass?" the mate demanded.

"North, northeast, but hold it into the wind or you'll upset her," the captain groaned.

Pigs Overboard

There was little comfort in these words, and I felt a tense feeling in the pit of my stomach. The captain told me to get some rest as there was nothing more I could do for him. With considerable difficulty I stumbled to my bunk near the forward entrance and found it soaked by spray which was periodically sweeping over the entire ship.

During one exceptionally large lurch the bow of the schooner actually submerged, washing twenty-five or thirty squealing pigs into the sea.

All the passengers who had been clinging to the top deck were noisily bedding down below on the aisle floor between the rows of bunks filled with flu-sick natives and the ever present scourge of seasickness. I was flung mercilessly against the side of the ship as it rolled, then out into the passageway on top of some unsuspecting victims as it rolled in the other direction.

More than once I had to clap my hand over my bloated cheeks to keep from anointing someone who was too sick or frightened to care anyway. I finally devised what seemed to me an ingenious way of bracing myself so I could become firmly lodged in my bunk and still reach the "sick bucket" tied to the bunk rail. No wonder they call us landlubber passengers *"hore patete,"* which translated literally means "bucket runners."

Prayer for Help

Prayer had occurred to me before, but there was so much confusion it seemed futile to try. But now the situation had worsened to such an extent it seemed necessary to pray if we were to survive. The words formed easily in my mind as I began to importune the throne of grace:

"O Lord, Master of wind and wave, thou knowest our plight. If this is the place thou hast designed to leave thy servant, let it be so. But if thou hast further work for us to do, please intervene in our behalf and save us, O Lord. We are surrounded by ignorance, superstition, and danger, and, oh, how feeble is our cry in attempting to correct these stubborn conditions. If it seemeth good unto thee, O God, lay bare thine almighty arm and minister unto us by thy matchless power. Thou who art Lord of the sea, still these gigantic waves if it be thy holy will. Thou who art controller of the elements, wield them now in our favor and burn a testimony of thy loving care into our consciousnesses. Thy will be done, O Lord, for we give ourselves completely into thy hands, in the name of thine Only Begotten Son, our Lord and Savior, Jesus Christ, even so, Amen."

I had become so engrossed in my petition I had hardly realized the ship had ceased to roll. I lay there for a few seconds conscious that the ship was on an even keel. I was almost afraid to move for fear it would begin to pitch and roll again. For fully five minutes I lay motionless in my bunk. A tingling of unquenchable joy was bursting inside me, but I dared not move. I realized something miraculous had transpired. Peace had settled over the ship. I sprang from my bunk, slid back the door, and crawled up over the spray-soaked copra sacks piled high on the foredeck and clambered over into the lifeboat lashed to the portside. The sky was clear, and gentle rolls had supplanted the frenzied sea that had battered us so mercilessly only a few minutes before.

I could see by the light of the brightest stars that the sea was slick as though some giant hand had smoothed it with a hot roller. The wind had shifted to the direction most beneficial to us, and the sailors were soon instructed to pull up the huge sails to take advantage of this added power which would now propel us with additional speed toward Tahiti.

We had not expected to reach home by Christmas Eve, but if these conditions persisted it was not out of the question. My heart was full of emotion and for over an hour I looked steadfastly into heaven and with moistening eyes thanked our heavenly Father for hearing our humble prayer. The rest of this night I spent in prayers of thanksgiving. This was a most powerful testimony to me, and I had the assurance that our heavenly Father was very near to us in this time of great peril.

On Course

The next day both passengers and crew marveled at the change which had so suddenly come upon us. The sick captain who had seldom shown himself above deck on the entire journey was now squatting on the top deck, sighting with the sextant to determine our true position.

"E mea maere roa," the captain said. He was completely baffled by the change that had taken place and was surprised to find that we were directly on course and that we had come so far in such a short while.

"I can't believe it, but it's true. I've checked the position twice. If we keep this up," the captain continued, "we will break all records on this run."

This was encouraging news to me, for I had resigned myself to the fact that I would not be with my family on Christmas Eve, or even for Christmas Day. Normally it would have been impossible, but this was not a normal experience

The Butterworth family aboard ship on one of their journeys to French Polynesia

Thrilling Experience

I said nothing of my testimony, for it seemed too precious to divulge to anyone. The day continued to be beautiful and even the sailors gathered around every few minutes to engage me in religious conversation. It was a thrilling experience, and several of the people suggested that the peaceful trip was probably due to my presence on board. This was the same old superstition we had been trying to counter but with a new twist, this time in reverse. This may have been a good time for me to bear testimony, but I kept silent. I knew I should tell them of my testimony, but for some reason I did not feel the ideal time had yet presented itself. The day closed and I sat alone far into the night communing with God and nature, anticipating our near approach to the main island. If all went well we were to arrive the next evening, Christmas Eve. I was looking steadfastly ahead into the darkness engaged in prayer of thanksgiving when I became suddenly aware that there was a rhythmic flash of light illuminating the ethereal formations high in the sky. At first I mistook this for lightning, but it was too mechanical for that. I waited until the sailor on watch came by and called it to his attention.

"Aue hoi e, te pou mori i Haapape." He ran excitedly to tell the captain who came immediately to investigate.

"That's the lighthouse at Haapape," the captain said. "We may reach Tahiti before morning."

Bearing Testimony

I could hardly contain the joy that welled up inside of me. I went down to my bunk and tried to sleep but found it impossible, for prayers of thanksgiving were continually forming in my mind. At the crack of dawn I was again on deck, and Tahiti was high out of the water on the right; Moorea, ten miles away, showed on the left. The ship was alive with activity, for when both of these islands are in sight we are very close to the harbor entrance at Papeete. I watched our Protestant friends who had blamed us for the ill winds on a previous journey, as they rolled and tied their belongings into a *peue* mat.

The deck was crowded with passengers and crew when the impression came to me to testify of our experience. I stated it briefly, but made the point that God had intervened or we may have perished. I expressed my deep concern that anyone would blame the Lord for deliberately provoking the elements to plague travelers at sea simply because missionaries were on board. I testified that this experience evidently came to us to counter that false opinion. I also testified that by sincere prayer we can lift ourselves to Him and receive protection in the hollow of his hand.

I arrived at the mission house before the family had aroused. They were surprised and overjoyed to have us arrive in time for the yuletide celebrations and to learn of the experience we had received.

We shared this marvelous experience at once with the Breckenridge family and bore testimony at the Tarona Wednesday evening prayer service, giving thanks and credit to our heavenly Father who stretched forth his powerful hand in our hour of need and showed us his wonderful love for suffering humanity.

Chapter 14

Ruins left by a tidal wave

Lost in a Tidal Wave

It was during the pearl-diving season at Hikueru in 1903 that a costly and frightening tidal wave destroyed hundreds of lives and caused untold property damage including a $10,000 loss of church property. Eyewitnesses said that although the village was situated on the highest point of land, it was suddenly inundated by a great watery mass which shook the whole atoll almost without warning.

Strangely enough the sun was still shining and the wind was at a dead calm. This, however, was only temporary, for suddenly a rush of wind shattered the windows of the little frame church towering among a cluster of low thatch-roofed houses. Those who were near by said the building seemed actually to bulge under the terrific wind pressure.

As the sun disappeared, a lead-colored sky turned midday into twilight. A sudden rain began driving horizontally, mixed with a sheet of stinging salt spray from the pounding surf.

Many Lives Lost

Stunned human beings frantically scurried for shelter. Some, more agile than others, climbed to the very tops of near-by coconut trees which proved to be a mortal mistake in many cases, for the added weight at the top of the tree caused the trunks to snap under the gale, or, with roots exposed by the churning waters below, were uprooted. A whole family was lost this way; as soon as the tree hit the ground another gigantic wave washed the human wreckage away forever.

A huge wave caught the church building broadside and flung it from its foundation. Succeeding waves sent it careening drunkenly until it was finally flung solidly against a half-dozen coconut trees. The impact of the crash dislodged many of the natives cowering high in the vibrating fronds above and felled them into the churning waters where no human being could survive. Later the church was seen half submerged floating in the lagoon.

Trees crisscrossed as they fell and the landscape was completely changed. Captain Lynch and three sailors off the copra schooner "Aorai" were clinging to the top of a tall coconut tree. The tree splintered about halfway up and the force of the wind carried the top of the tree and its human fruit several hundred feet before it struck the lagoon. They were killed instantly.

It was necessary to take to the trees, as the sea was breaking furiously over the whole terrain and the crushing logs and debris would soon make short work of human sinew. It was difficult to breathe, in fact almost impossible except by pressing the lips close to the tree trunks. The safest

142

place seemed for one to be lashed to a tree trunk just above the watermarks, preferably to a tree that had already been shorn of its top and with some protection near the roots. It is important, as experience taught these people, that one should not climb too high, for the added weight only increases the hazard of uprooting the tree.

Fresh Water

The storm at Hikueru lasted until three in the morning when its fury was finally spent. Missionary J. W. Gilbert and Mr. Alexander Drollet took a census in the morning and found that only three hundred of the original one thousand or more inhabitants remained alive. These survivors actually owed their lives to Brother Gilbert and Mr. Drollet. Brother Gilbert had some knowledge of chemistry, and with the support of Mr. Drollet he set to work to distill sea water in order to quench the thirst of the entire population.

All fresh water supplies had been destroyed. Brother Gilbert found a large boiler in the debris, evidently from the wreckage of a copra schooner. He set it on two wet logs and filled it with sea water. A hollow bedstead was used as a pipe from the boiler to the condenser. The condenser was merely shielding of corrugated roofing around the pipe extending from the boiler. The distillery was set up beside a natural water hole, and from this hole brackish water was handed to a man standing on a stool beside the condenser who poured the water over the pipe to condense fresh water more quickly. The first day, six barrels of sea water produced but a bucketful of fresh water. This was divided among the workers and children. A second distillery was devised and the output of fresh water was greatly increased until the rains came. It was a day of rejoicing, and Brother Gilbert had become a hero.

A Second Tidal Wave

In 1958 another tidal wave lashed out at the peaceful little islands in the dangerous archipelago. Brother Allen Breckenridge and I were making a routine visit to the phosphate island of Makatea. For several days the sea had been unusually high, but otherwise the weather was fine.

One evening I was sitting by the radio set with Avivi a Turi, former pastor and governor of the island and our congenial host during our visit to Makatea. We both heard a radio report in the native language which warned of a tidal wave approaching from the Marquesas and that it would arrive in two days. We called to Brother Breckenridge who had just gone upstairs and told him what we had heard.

"We must cable home right away," Allen said. "Jane seldom listens to the radio when I'm away and may not have heard that report." We were very concerned about this, because a tidal wave from the Marquesas would hit Tarona full force, since it is at sea level and a little below sea level in places.

The phosphate island of Makatea

Cable to Papeete

I agreed that we should send a cable right away. Makatea, because of the phosphate works, is one of the few islands with the luxury of cable connections. We worded our cables very carefully and took them to the T.S.F. station. The operator did not want to send them, arguing that he was also the weatherman for the island and no such report had come to him.

"But I heard the report myself," I pleaded. "We're concerned about our families at Papeete who may get caught off guard. We just want to warn them."

"You know the consequences of false weather reports," he said. "Why don't you let me contact the weather office at Papeete for you, and I'll let you know what the score really is."

"Do it right away," we demanded, and left feeling relieved, for we felt that he would surely receive the report of the tidal wave from Papeete. It was some time later that a runner brought us a cablegram received from the weather bureau at Papeete. It was written on an official cablegram and signed by the local meteorological officer at Makatea who received the report. The report said that no tidal wave warnings had been received or disseminated.

"Are you sure you heard that report, Eddie?" Allen asked.

"There's my witness," I said, pointing to Avivi. "He heard it, too."

"Yes, it's true," Avivi added. "It was a real report all right."

"That settles it," Allen said. "Let's send the cables."

On the Alert

The radio officer was surprised to see us again after having sent us the report that all was calm.

We demanded that the messages be sent and took all the responsibility if shipping schedules were disrupted in any way by our report. Reluctantly he sent the messages as we had requested. At Papeete the reception of these cables by our families caused quite a stir.

We have a very good and trusted French friend, Dr. C. A. Wurfel, on whom we depend for advice and counsel on many different phases of life in a French country. He is also our family medical adviser. When I am out of town, Lilly Raye usually contacts him for help with any difficult problems that arise. This was one of those times. She and Jane went out to his house and read the cable to him. He immediately called the weather office and confirmed the former report sent to us at Makatea that no tidal wave report had been received. But it was a comfort to us at Makatea that the family had been warned and were on the alert.

The next day Allen and I walked along the Makatea seashore among the houses of the phosphate workmen and told some of the people that a tidal wave had been reported and would arrive in two days. This report must have sounded strange to them, for it was a perfect day. We even joked about our impetuousness of sending the cablegrams when no one else seemed to be worrying about it. The sea was more calm now than it had been at any time during the past several weeks.

Tidal wave debris left in a coconut grove

Here It Comes

But on the evening of the second day the wind began to rise. At church time it had reached almost hurricane force, but only in gusts every few seconds. We opened the service with the usual song and prayer, and I chose for my Scripture the words of the Lord in the Doctrine and Covenants (43:6), "How oft have I called upon you by the mouth of my servants . . . and by the voice of thunderings, and by the voice of lightnings, and by the voice of tempests, and by the voice of earthquakes, and great hailstorms, and by the voice of famines and pestilences of every kind . . ." There was a powerful spirit present, and we were impressed to say that the voice of the Lord in these elements was crying repentance. Trees and large limbs were falling all around and the congregation was restless, but we continued the service the full time allotted.

We had to pick our way home over fallen trees, and one tree had fallen on a house directly in front of ours, crushing the roof. It was not until the next day that we learned about the tidal wave. The little village was almost completely wiped out.

We walked along the shore where only the day before scores of houses had stood, but now only an occasional cement cistern was left to mark the location of the house.

As we walked among the wreckage and debris left by the tidal wave, the strange radio report we had heard two days earlier kept echoing in our ears. Makatea suffered the brunt of the tidal wave, and we were glad we had spread the word, for many lives were no doubt spared because people were on the alert. About a week later we returned to Papeete and found that it had got only the backlash of the wave, but that Tarona had been covered by about six or eight inches of water.

Avivi a Turi, our host at Makatea, had made arrangements with us to go to the island of Borabora for a series of missionary meetings in his son's home. We had planned to go by plane from Papeete the following week. The day before we were supposed to leave, a cable from Honolulu arrived. Brother David Kaleikau and his family were newly appointed missionaries to Tahiti and had sent us notice that they would arrive within the week. This forced us to cancel our arrangements to go to Borabora.

We went to see Avivi the day before he left and canceled our trip. Avivi left the next morning and was killed in a plane crash at Raiatea. Fifteen passengers were lost on this ill-fated trip, which we were averted from taking only by a very slight turn of events.

Chapter 15

"Limping Lena," the missionary bus

Limping Lena

The sun rises early in the tropics and the household usually begins to stir about six o'clock. Lilly Raye gave us a choice of hot wheat cereal, bacon and eggs, pancakes, or waffles. I ruled out the hot wheat cereal on the grounds that it was too much work grinding the wheat, and besides it was getting moldy. Gary said the bacon had too much gristle in it, and Cheryl and Janis hated the large specks on the eggs which they called "chicken eyes." By the time we had all agreed on waffles, Lilly Raye already had the pancakes sizzling on the griddle.

Our usual morning fruit was *pomplemouse,* a quality grapefruit unknown outside the tropics. We had but to step out on the back porch to pluck bananas nearly a foot long from a perpetual stalk hung there by our yard attendant Terii Samuela, and plucked from a grove growing on the back of the property at Tarona.

Following breakfast and *Daily Bread* devotions, Lilly Raye took turns with Jane Breckenridge driving the children to the Mamao School in our little French "Simca." French schools start at 7:30 a.m. and run until 11:30 a.m., with two short recesses. The noon hour is from 11:30 until 2:00 and ostensibly is to cover the traditional siesta period.

Our usual duties consist of office work, housework, counseling, receipt writing, an occasional administration, except during frequent epidemics when this activity keeps us going almost constantly. Much of our time is spent in translating materials for sermons, classwork, or for the local church paper *Te Orometua* which is sent out from the mission office to several hundred subscribers. The wife of the missionary also translates materials for the women's work in which Lilly Raye and Jane are very active. Lilly Raye had a triple load which made it necessary to hire a native maid to do the menial household chores. She taught piano and organ to the Tarona young people, did the mission secretarial work, and handled the bishop's books, jobs which are generally required of the wife of the mission president.

For several years we maintained an orchestra of about twenty-five pieces which took a lot of time for individual instruction. The high point in the history of our orchestra was its appearance at a public concert held at the local hospital at which the governor of Tahiti and many of the local officials were present. We were the envy of the islands in our blue and gold uniforms donated to us by Graceland College. The orchestra finally disbanded, and the hats were sold to the local police force whose members still wear them on formal occasions.

Girls' Chorus

Lilly Raye spent a lot of time organizing and instructing a girls' chorus from among the younger

"L'Orchestre Sanito" directed by Brother Butterworth for several years in Tahiti

girls of the mission. They were able to attain a very high quality of musicianship and became the basic unit around which a fine choir was finally organized. The girls' chorus practiced twice a week which made it easy for the choir to pick up new pieces when they came together with the chorus.

The zenith attainment of the choir came during the joint ministry with Alan and Gladys Tyree. Lilly Raye and Gladys alternated on the organ and piano under the general direction of Alan. The choir presented a public soiree at the local theater, which was attended by the governor and his staff. We feel that this was well received and we were encouraged by the reports and the statement of the governor himself after the concert. The ladies of the choir wore beautiful pastel formal dresses, while the men were dressed in pure white including the bow ties. We sang a high quality of music in several languages the first

153

The Alan Tyree family, still in French Polynesia

part of the program, then a more informal program of instrumental and special numbers the last half; these also were very well done. This would have been more difficult had we not had the former KLDS Stone Church radio organ which is now installed at Tarona.

In 1958 the Tarona girls' chorus was selected as a basic unit around which a city-wide Red Cross program was organized by Mr. Gérard Müller. The girls performed superbly and were the high light of the program when they sang an original verse about Tahiti:

> Te tiare no 'ano'a roa,
> Te tiare ïa no Tahiti.
> Maerehia te anuanua,
> I te aï'a here, i Tahiti.
> E te ava'e, ua maramarama;
> E te himene, ua navenave mau.
> Uihi â te mata'i mărû
> I te fenua ra i Tahiti.

The Tarona Saints are known all over French Polynesia for their high-quality hymn singing, and on Wednesday evenings in particular, many non-member friends may be found in the churchyard listening to the singing.

So goes the ordinary activities on the main island. But this was no ordinary day, for today the *manu reva* was to arrive at 1:30 p.m. The sky bird, called *"avion"* by the French, would bring mail from all over the world to this anxious little villa in the heart of the Pacific Ocean. Only a few years earlier this mode of travel was unknown to the natives of French Polynesia. We used to wait three months for the arrival of the "Thor I," which made mail day a very colorful occasion. The mad throngs near the post office were almost as entertaining as a festive street scene in gay *Paree,* nor has this lessened much even though mail comes more regularly now. On a day such as this all work stops, and letters from home are the main topic of conversation for the rest of the day. Letter writing and reading usually kept us busy for several days.

The noon meal was ordinarily a light lunch of sandwiches, salad, and fruit, with a lime drink or tropical thirst-quenching punch, or more recently, milk, since Tahiti now boasts a large dairy called "Sachet" which is equipped to pasteurize *du lait.* We had three bottles a day delivered to our door. Formerly we took milk from a family who belonged to the church, and the milk was delivered by a leper boy. We did not know it at the time,

155

but he was later confined to the leper colony. The milk was delivered in large liter bottles used originally by the brewing company. The caps were usually funneled leaves which were stuck in stopper-wise. A vivid memory of our own pasteurization attempts was the inevitable overflowing kettle and mopping up of scorched milk foam.

Tuna Fish

A favorite evening meal was fresh tuna fish served with steaming boiled *umara* or sweet potatoes. We favored tomato paste sauce rather than gravy made from flour if the sauce was garnished with chopped onions. Breadfruit baked on an open charcoal fire made of dry coconut husks was a very satisfying meal resembling a cross between a mealy potato and a squash.

Portable organ used in the Islands for many years

Somehow the preparation of tuna fish became a head-of-the-house chore. After numerous experiments we devised an easy method of peeling off the slick blue skin. We found that it was easy to do if we began near the gills and peeled uniformly toward the tail fins. Slicing down the spine beside the vertical bones until we reached the horizontal bones in the center of the fish, we could lift out four quarters of dark boneless meat that had but to be sliced and arranged in the freezing compartment. Tuna is a warm-blooded fish, and a more delicious meat is hard to find. It compares favorably to beefsteak. This is similarly true of turtle steaks which we had as an occasional delicacy.

The evenings were spent in various ways. A family car ride around dusk was the usual thing when we were on the main island of Tahiti. We would tour the city; or if a tourist boat was docked, we would drive down to the wharf where we could revel momentarily in the luxury of modern tourists. Sometimes in the cool of the evening we would tour the entire one hundred mile circumference of Tahiti itself, stopping at the famous Chinese restaurant at Taravao fifty miles away from Papeete. At Taravao the restaurant owner would invite us into the kitchen so we could point out the food we wanted as it steamed enticingly on the gigantic wood range in large iron kettles.

Regularly during the week we had young people's meeting, prayer meetings, and women's meetings at the Tarona church or in the homes. We were sometimes asked to assist in home visiting and more particularly in missionary meetings held twice a week in the outer districts around the main island. The power lines reached only to the near-by districts of Faaa and Arue, so we had to generate our own electricity with small portable units when we ventured beyond these limits.

"Limping Lena"

Tarona owned a missionary bus, affectionately called "Limping Lena" by the missionaries. It was usually loaded with volunteer workers who not only looked forward to the ride into the district but actually enjoyed pioneering in the establishment of new missions around the main island. The initial meetings were usually held in the open air under the graceful palms, but in certain seasons we were foiled by the inclemency of the weather. This usually prompted the friends of the church to volunteer to help us build a temporary thatch building where services could be held without molestation by the unruly elements.

We usually made a small charge for passengers going on the missionary run to the district, but this did not insure them that they would not have to push old Limping Lena a kilometer or so somewhere along the line. It was only on the rare occasion, or the odd time as the Canadians would say, that Limping Lena would lie right down in the middle of the road and force us to thumb our

*The author, typing this story, sits
outside the mission house in Tahiti*

way home. My memories of Limping Lena can
be summed up in a very few words, "Oh, my
aching back!"

Chapter 16

The Kon-Tiki

The Kon-Tiki Arrives

Tumureva a Kamake was peering steadfastly into the black night which hung deathlike over the circular lagoon. Why should this strange light blink at him so steadily? It was not a fire. He had seen fires many times as the villagers worked the copra groves on the opposite side of the lagoon eight miles away. This was no ordinary fire; besides, it was off season for gathering copra for that section, and anyone camping out in a closed *rahui* is subject to prosecution. Being a Polynesian the first thought occurring to him was of the supernatural. He watched for several minutes, then shook his head and turned quickly away. Maybe he was imagining things. He rubbed his eyes and glanced back over his shoulder. The light was still there. He was too frightened to share his singular experience with anyone. He took his guitar and sat down on the ground behind the hut facing away from the mysterious flashing light. Music always seems to still the troubled Polynesian spirit. For two nights in a row he saw this light appear, disappear, then suddenly reappear again, always in the same spot. It had a peculiar glow, so different from anything he had yet seen on Raroia, one of the outer fringe islands in the dangerous archipelago.

Early one morning as several bronze-skinned children were splashing in the warm lagoon surf, they discovered some strange floating objects gently nudging the piers of the small improvised wharf as the movement of the restless lagoon forced them shoreward. These objects were gathered by the children and taken quickly to the village chief who immediately called an emergency *apooraa* of all the villagers.

"The *'tamarii* have found some very oddly shaped tins," the chief said. "I think we should open them and examine the contents."

The ever-inquisitive natives drew closer to get a better look. A huge knife was brought and with a wave of his hand the chief ordered his teen-age son to open the tins. It was a crude job, but the contents of the tins divulged that some very strange inhabitants had descended on the quiet village; for this food was different from any they had ever seen.

"It is certain," the chief continued, "that somewhere along the rim of the reef a foreign yacht has met an untimely end. We must organize a searching party at once."

Shortly a score of outriggers and motorboats were gathered at the wharf awaiting final instructions.

"Could my brother and I try searching that area?" Tumureva did not explain why, but he pointed in the direction of the strange light he had seen a few nights earlier.

"Yes," the chief answered, "but don't all of you go in the same direction. We have thirty miles of reef to search."

The natives spread out quickly in all directions and began searching diligently, for there is always a generous reward from the French government to all those who help a ship in distress. Tumureva had a fast outrigger with a ten-foot sail. It was a still day, and they had to tack, but in thirty minutes they were within sight of the area where Tumureva had seen the light. Through the sparse coconut grove they could see a strange heap of logs and plaited bamboo lying haphazardly on the reef. Several pup tents were here and there on the sandy beach. Six tall men, some with grizzly beards, were waving frantically at them. These were no ordinary men. There was no yacht, there were no floating masts, no conventional wood of any kind usually associated with a shipwreck. What manner of men were these?

Tumureva tightened the sail and turned the outrigger back from the shore. Outrigger arm high out of the water, he sailed by several times at high speed to get a closer look. Tumureva watched for signs of guns, spears, or other weapons. The visitors had only the usual number of arms and legs, so they were evidently not visitors from outer space. Tumureva finally caught sight of the familiar French flag hanging in a position of honor from a coconut tree, then he noticed that the cloth they had been waving from a long pole was another

Mr. Bengt Danielsson and his wife
and daughter. Man on right is
son-in-law of John Mervin

kind of flag. This gave Tumureva and his brother
courage to go ashore, for these were evidently
friendly visitors. All fear was abolished when
they heard the friendly greeting *"Ia ora na,"* Polynesian words meaning "May you have life." After
a few minutes of sign language and attempts at
conversation, it was decided that Mr. Bengt Danielsson, one of the members of the Kon-Tiki expedition, should go with Tumureva to the other
side of the lagoon for a talk with the chief. This
was done and soon the whole village was alive
with inquisitive eagerness.

The next day the lagoon was white with sails
all heading toward the land-fall area. It had been
arranged that the whole village would help drag

164

the Kon-Tiki off the reef into the lagoon. After considerable difficulty the raft and all six members of the expedition were safe in the hospitable village of Raroia. Typical welcome festivities had long since been under way. The formal welcome was by dancing, speechmaking, and singing. One of the songs sung by the villagers which fairly reverberated through the copra grove was the greeting song which has since become known as the Kon-Tiki song. It goes like this:

Terai ma te ata	Terai from the cloud world
To revaraa mai e,	Your singular arrival.
Na te moana	Over the ocean
Patitifa e,	Pacific,
Aue hoi te aroha e.	Oh, how great the joy.
Tono e to huiraatira!	Go, villagers!
Tavere mai ia Kon-	Pull the Kon-Tiki off the
Tiki e.	reef.

Two years later, Mr. Bengt Danielsson and his wife, Marie-Therese, returned to Kon-Tiki Island to take up temporary residence for the purpose of writing a story about this happy island. The coconut which had been brought to Raroia from Peru tied to the bottom of the Kon-Tiki raft had grown during the interim to a height of three feet. The natives had not changed much and were overjoyed to see *Penetito* return to their island. Mr. Danielsson had returned to live with these people and to study their customs. For several months they were isolated on this lonely island. It was during one of our routine trips to the Outer Archipelago that Brother Breckenridge and I landed on the Raroian atoll. We did not know at the time that Mr. Danielsson was living there. We had taken refuge within the Raroia reef enclosure from a serious storm at sea. We were entertained by the Danielssons who seemed delighted that we had come. We later learned that we were the first *popaa* or white people to visit the island since their arrival. At midnight on the first day of our arrival I was suddenly awakened out of a deep sleep. In the dim lamplight I found myself staring full into the face of a bearded man who was shaking me gently and mumbling something that did not seem intelligible at the time due to the startling manner in which I was awakened.

"Mr. Butterworth, Mr. Butterworth," he called, "please come with me quickly."

I got up hurriedly and after I was fully aroused questioned him about the urgency of the situation.

"A woman is about to give birth, and she is in need of medicine." Bengt asked me what medicines I had brought with me. A quick look in the kit showed a good supply of penicillin, various miracle drug pills, ether, bandages, and aspirin. We went to the small hut and by the time we had arrived, the child was born.

"I have a new solution," I said, "which Dr. Wurfel advises we put in the baby's eyes immediately after it is born. This will keep down the incidence of ophthalmia neonatorum, gonorrhea of the eyes." So many children are born blind or are blinded soon after birth because of this terrible infection so prevalent in the islands. (One estimate sets the infection rate at between 80 and 90 per cent of the native population.)

Roping Sea Turtles

On the following day a large sea turtle was discovered by the sharp eyes of some of the natives who are usually scanning the sea. They spotted a floating object some distance offshore and yelled *honu* to alert the fishermen who are never far away. Several young fishermen sprang from their pallets and grabbed ropes, oars, and diving goggles on the way to the outrigger. They shoved off and paddled furiously in the direction of the floating object. One of the young men dived from his outrigger and splashed headlong into the sea a few feet behind the turtle. The sluggish reptile dived to seek shelter in deeper water, but by this time the native was astride its enormous back. The fin flippers were thrashing the water into a foam as its captor trapped one fin between his shoulder and neck while holding the other flipper under the turtle. The powerful downstroke of the flipper cannot be held back by an ordinary man, but the upstroke is easily prevented. While one fin is held down, the other will automatically stay up but it can be serious if it flaps the diver in the face. For this reason the flippers are held in this manner. This leaves one arm free to slip a rope over one flipper of the turtle and then to swim back to the canoe. He may have been carried far under water or a long way from the outrigger, but generally the rope is long enough to reach the necessary length.

The turtle is then drawn toward shore by pulling the rope behind the outrigger. Once ashore the turtle is examined to see if it is large enough to purchase for a community feast (some turtles weigh over five hundred pounds). We were standing near by when the deal was closed and it was decided that it would be butchered immediately and made ready for the earth oven. Two native boys pulled the turtle into the meager shade of a coconut tree, washed the undershell with a douse of sea water and started to carve up the turtle in a very merciless manner.

"Aren't you going to kill it first?" I asked.

"No," was the reply. "If we kill it first it will be so tough we can't eat it, and we don't have very good teeth as you can see."

I cannot describe the feeling that surged through my conscience as I stood by and made a movie of the whole primitive butchering job. The turtle gasped and wheezed but made no other audible sound. Since they are not snapping turtles it made no attempt to attack its murderers. I had seen many primitive things done by these people, but this was the cruelest thing I had ever seen.

Getting ready for the turtle feast a native *tahu'a* began an eerie fire chant as he rubbed a *burau* branch down the center rib of a dry coconut frond. There was a wisp of smoke, followed seconds later by a burst of flame. I could not eat the flesh after having watched the barbarous slaughter, but I was evidently the only one so affected. I did, however, purchase the beautiful shell and after varnishing it to a high

Dr. Karl Wurfel and his wife,
and Mrs. Butterworth

sheen, put it on the wall of my den as a grim reminder of our sojourn in this primitive aboriginal society.

Eating Live Fish

The eating of raw still-twitching fish was another evidence that we were in a very distant world, but the manner in which these fish were caught was an interesting study in the development of primeval minds. They stripped down the leaves from a long coconut palm and twisted them together making a rude but very effective net. These nets were in use long before the white man discovered the existence of this teeming brown race on these storybook islands.

We watched them drag hundreds of smeltlike fish to the rim of the lagoon, then saw them catch the fish with their bare hands and throw them out on the shore to be picked up by the families waiting there for their portion. This type of *hukilau* fishing is generally a village project where men, women, and children help out as best they can and take enough fish to last them for several days. To keep them fresh, they weave small baskets in which the fish are kept alive submerged in the lagoon near the hut. Usually once a week the *hukilau* ceremony, which takes on the tenor of a joyous fete, is enacted in a spirit of hilarity. It seemed more like a game than the pursuit of a steady occupation.

To keep in practice in the use of throwing the spear, they participate on special days in a very ancient game which they call *patiaraa fa*. A coconut is raised on a twenty-foot pole implanted firmly in the ground. Another identical target is placed about a hundred feet away. The idea of the game is not necessarily to hit the nut, but to lodge the spear high on the nut. The highest spear wins the prize. They are surprisingly accurate with the spear, and while I watched, the spears just barely missed as they skimmed over the tiptop of the target. The winner of the contest received the yellow box from which I had taken the film to record their maneuvers.

These were only some of the strange happenings we witnessed on Kon-Tiki Island. There was a tug of sadness on our hearts as the beautiful sunset announced the near departure of our copra schooner. The storm had subsided and the wind was nearly normal again, but the sea was still rough. While on the island, we had revived our small branch and erected a picturesque assembly building made of plaited coconut thatch. We held services every night and left with the feeling that our ministry had been well received. We took our reluctant leave amidst tears of genuine concern and sincere sorrow, for these days had been filled with entertainment, education in native culture, and with an abundance of strange happenings on Raroia, now known throughout French Polynesia as Kon-Tiki Island.

Chapter 17

*A typical Polynesian, and a
church member*

Strange Customs

One of the most thrilling rides I have ever experienced in French Polynesia was aboard an American racing yacht in the fall of 1957. Mr. Bengt Danielsson of Kon-Tiki fame and author of many books on Polynesian lore had arranged for me to accompany an expedition from Stanford University as interpreter and business manager while in the Tuamotu. I was also the go-between for the American captain who spoke no native and his sailors who understood little English.

Tacking or changing over from motor to sail power was always a crisis. The captain would shout orders I didn't even understand, let alone attempt to translate into Tahitian. I never knew there were so many curse words in the English language, but in the native tongue these all resolve into "pig" and "dog" anyway so I didn't bother to interpret literally.

At tacking time, the fifty-foot sails towering high overhead had to be changed over to the opposite side of the ship. This meant we had to turn the ship so the sails would go momentarily limp in the breeze, and in the few seconds before the ship had turned into the wind again, all sails and ropes had to be secured. This was difficult to do in such a short time and only a slight miscalculation could overturn the yacht. I can still visualize Captain Stan with one knee curled over the tiller, ropes in both hands, and maybe occasionally a rope between his teeth.

We listed between thirty and forty-five degrees all the time due to the pull of the windjammed sails. In one rough sea we took on so much water we had about six inches of bilge water all over the cabin floor. I had the feeling we were sinking, but somehow for three days of this torture we managed to stay afloat. We were now approaching what appeared to be a Tuamotuan atoll.

The tiny island of Apataki has a very wide pass and having been here many times before, I was able to act as pilot until we were safely made fast to the cement wharf. About thirty or forty members of the church were on hand to give us a royal welcome. At a community meeting later on, I acted as interpreter for the expedition spokesman who explained the purpose of our visit. We had come to photograph undersea marine life on 35 mm. color movie film. We organized crews of divers and utility men, including outriggers and sailors to man them. We used our own church members as much as possible.

Our biggest production was the filming of an actual pearl-diving scene using Elder Nui Arahu as star performer. Nui is a jovial, rotund man of about sixty years of age who lives up to his name "charcoal." His sonorous voice and pleasant demeanor make him the sought-after spokesman for all formal occasions involving visiting dignitaries.

We Become Doctors

One evening at the mission house while a dinner of tern eggs and French fried breadfruit chips was being served the captain and four members of the University Expedition, we were interrupted by a commotion outside. An excited crowd was running toward a thatch hut about two hundred yards away. Soon a native runner informed me that a serious accident had occurred and that we were needed immediately. The captain and I excused ourselves and left hurriedly.

My medical kit was pretty well stocked for routine calls, but this was not routine. The frail form of a boy about ten with a gaping ten-inch gash across his chest was lying on the floor. We could see his little heart beating between the exposed ribs under a very thin tissue. The skin had evidently been ripped. A whole army of natives were in action doing all they knew to do. One group was out frantically chopping down banana stalks. These stalks were delivered to another nervous group who beat them into pulp, using heavy stones. A third group grabbed the mangled stalks and rushed to the victim's side to wring out the juice directly on the wound, with pulp and dirt falling into the open wound.

"What a terrible primitive way to treat the lad," the captain said. "He'll die if we don't do something."

"What happened?" I demanded, trying to find someone calm enough to talk with me. I finally

Nordly's yacht, used on ride to Apataki

learned that he was sliding down a coconut tree and got hung up on a rusty nail.

We finally succeeded in getting them to let us take over. We elevated him on a small table spread with a clean white cloth, but he protested our every move vigorously and started the blood flowing again. It was apparent we would have to put him under anesthesia. I was the only one he would allow to come near him, and this was probably because I could speak Tahitian. By this time the other members of the expedition had come to investigate. We made a formidable looking clinic in this primitive setting, but we didn't exude much confidence in our ability to handle the task cut out for us.

I tried to visualize the situation through the eyes of the child. The captain was a rough looking character, but actually he was gentle. His reddish goatee and long shaggy sideburns were the most frightening things about him. The expedition cameramen were a Mutt and Jeff pair who kept up a constant prattle in English, a strange tongue to the little patient. The two female members of the expedition were dressed in gaudy Western attire and looked decidedly out of place in this setting.

It fell my lot to soak the cotton with ether and coax the boy to let us put him to sleep. He was soon fast asleep, and we went to work cleaning the wound, suturing and dusting with sulfa powder. We gave him an injection of tetanus antitoxin, and after about thirty minutes the deed was done. The corps of self-appointed specialists had done their work with surprisingly good results.

Time for Prayer

One of the cameramen made a startling statement, "Reverend, we have done all we can humanly do, but this little lad needs a good prayer to go along with this operation." I had wanted to administer to the lad, but had hesitated with so many around. The time was now ripe for such a procedure, so as the room became quiet we bowed in humble adoration and administered to the afflicted lad. We were the heros of Apataki and have since learned that the scar on our little patient can hardly be seen.

We were ill-equipped to treat the other cases we discovered on the island of Apataki, but we were able to diagnose them fairly accurately by referring to our Mercks manual. We found several cases of tuberculosis, peptic ulcer, and some fever diseases carried by those unseen invectors riding on diaphanous wings. The most horrible of these was elephantiasis, a lymph gland disorder caused by the invasion of filaria.

On one occasion we helped extract the multitined snout of a needlefish that had broken off in the shoulder of a young lad. We gave dozens of penicillin shots but were very ineffective against the outbreak of polio which struck the island for the first time while we were there. It is singular, however, that no paralytic cases developed from those who were given penicillin.

For our work on Apataki we were given a beautiful pair of vini birds—deep blue colored parakeets. My son Gary trained one of these to do several tricks. The bird was his constant companion until we left the Islands in 1958.

The local branch at Apataki gave our expedition a royal farewell typical of island hospitality, and the members of the expedition have never forgotten that strange island and its unusual customs. A donation of 5,000 francs was made by the leader of the expedition. The islanders stated their desire that the money be used as a nest egg for the local building fund.

Chapter 18

Shipwrecked boat on a reef

Shipwreck on the Reef

Passing through the Tuamotuan Archipelago, one is impressed by the surprising number of ghost-ship skeletons which still shudder and creek upon impact of the incessant sea as it crashes over the coral reef. Nearly every island can point to a spot or two where some unwary copra schooners met their untimely doom. From a vantage point on shore or from a secure ship deck one cannot know the horrors connected with a floundering ship.

The Apostle Paul, prisoner on a wheat freighter in Asia Minor, suffered shipwreck, but the experience meant little to me until I myself suffered shipwreck on a lonely coral reef in the dangerous archipelago.

It should not have come as a complete surprise to me, for by premonition some weeks earlier I was forewarned of some mishap which would befall me. I think the premonition was necessary to prepare me for the shock that was to be mine and to give me assurance that my heavenly Father would be by my side in that hour of need.

Something Is Wrong

One tropical evening, just as the blazing sun was about to dip below the horizon, Tihoni Mervin, captain of the "Hiro," stopped by the island of Kaukura to take on several tons of copra. I had just finished a series of missionary meetings on Kaukura and had been waiting for a passing schooner to take me to Papeete. When I came aboard I met Tihoni at the wheelhouse holding nervously to the tiller. Usually when standing near the reef the captain himself will hold the tiller. He seemed worried about something, so I did not engage in lengthy conversation with him.

It was long after sundown before we pulled away from the island of Kaukura. Some hours later when we were far out to sea the ship began acting curiously. It seemed to be going in a wide arc no matter what pressure was exerted on the tiller. Brother Mervin knew immediately what had happened. We had lost our rudder. He confided in me that he had known it was loose, but he hoped we could get back to Papeete to fix it since there was no way to fix it at sea. He asked me to keep the news from the other passengers in order to avoid panic.

Fortunately, the "Hiro" was one of the few ships in French Polynesia with a double screw propeller operated by dual motors. This made it possible for us to keep on a direct course by skillfully alternating the speeds of the propellers.

The only danger we now faced was the possibility of one motor giving out or of encountering an exceptionally rough sea. The barometer was momentarily steady, but there were earlier reports of bad weather ahead. We were several hundred miles from Tahiti and our speed had necessarily been cut down to allow for time to maneuver the motors. Brother Mervin sat by the wheelhouse in his canvas deck chair, keeping his eyes both on the compass and on the motion of the sea. It seemed strange that no one was holding the tiller in such a rough sea. I stood by and watched the strange proceedings for some time and finally retired to my bunk.

Nightmare

During the restless sleep which periodically came I experienced a suffocating nightmare, unlike anything I had ever experienced. The cabin seemed to be filling with water until I was completely covered. I was frozen to my pallet, powerless to move. As the water closed over me I could hear someone say, "He's gone! He's gone!" I awakened with a terrified feeling and sprang from my bunk fully expecting to find the ship in dire peril. On deck, however, everything was calm, and Tihoni was dozing in his deck chair. The maneuvering had now taken on a familiar pattern, and the two native boys knew exactly how to send the signals to the engine room.

Somehow the dream was too real to get out of my mind. I knew there was some reason it had been impressed upon me. It crossed my mind that it was to prepare me to be calm in the face of disaster.

I fell into deep thought as to what I would say as the ship was going down so there would not be panic on board. How could we prepare to meet impending fate? I told no one of the experience. For one whole day I fasted and prayed, keeping constant vigil as to the moment of our disaster. Each unnatural lurch of the ship brought me bolt upright, but calm and collected. It was almost disappointing that I could not demonstrate my new found powers of facing danger in such confidence.

About noon of the following day, the green mountaintops of Tahiti burst into view through the haze. The whole ship came alive with joy at the impressive sight. Elder John Mervin had successfully maneuvered the "Hiro" expertly over several hundred miles of deserted sea without a rudder; but what was even more impressive was to watch this "son of the sea" take that bulky ship through a dangerous pass at the Papeete harbor and along a very narrow channel, to tie up at the Papeete wharf without incident. We had arrived safely.

A few weeks later I was on board the small copra schooner "Haupea," captained by another member of the church, Alfred Richmond, uncle of Thérèse Richmond now at Graceland College. It was a moonless night and we were passing between the islands of Tikehau and Rairoa.

Shipwreck

During the night we were to pass over the hulk of the renowned gospel boat "Te Evanelia" which is mentioned in the Doctrine and Covenants. Naturally my thoughts turned to the history of that frail craft which lay fathoms below on the ocean floor, covered with barnacles and crustaceans of another kingdom. During the pre-engine period former missionaries for the church, Brother and Sister Joseph Burton and Brother and Sister Hubert Case, sailed this small ship to Polynesia.

My missionary life seemed easy in comparison to that difficult period. Here I sat on the rear deck of a motor-driven vessel, eating raw peanuts from one of several two-hundred-pound sacks piled high around us to keep the spray off the helmsman. Our trolling line had been forgotten and we had been pulling a large dead fish for several hours. When this was discovered, one of the natives said with a trace of sincere superstition that it was an ill omen.

About nine o'clock I retired to my bunk and was soon fast asleep. The ship lurched unnaturally. I had the same terrified feeling I had had before, but I had not yet connected this with the premonition of several weeks earlier. The thought of sinking entered my mind, and the picture seemed to be slowly taking shape. The only thing now was that I could not remember the final outcome of the dream. Would we be lost or saved? But one thing for sure was certain, the calmness of the situation for which I had previously fasted and prayed was now mine.

The ship was being literally crushed to death on the reef. It was tossed mercilessly at all angles, and we were being banged around with exceptional roughness. The railing around the back deck was crushed when the ship was turned on its side and forced by the waves against the reef. When the waves receded, the ship bounced back at almost an equivalent angle in the opposite direction. No one can imagine how terrifying this can be, but despite the confusion I was calm and collected. The captain was giving unintelligible orders, but no one was listening. With fright in his eyes he came to me to ask what we should do. I had already thought this out. I told him to get a twelve-inch plank and tie it to the rear of the ship in order to keep the propeller away from the reef. If the propeller were driven through the bottom of the boat it would drown out the engine room and douse the lights. We were being slammed around so mercilessly the sailors never did get the plank in place.

Finally the inevitable happened. We were now in total darkness. The captain told me to jump ashore, but it was too black out there to know where to jump. He flashed his small light to show the way, but it seemed too dangerous to jump. He told me three times to jump, for if the ship sank (one side of the ship was already crushed and thirty-eight tons of copra spilled from it) we would be sucked under.

The previous dream was now full of meaning for me. I needed to jump in order to pave the way and help the others to safety. None of the sailors would jump first, so I stepped up on the

*This was the bed made on the
rocky reef after the wreck*

ricketey railing and when the waves tipped us over
again I jumped. I could not see that the railing
was covered with oil which caused me to lose
force in the jump, and I fell into the chilling sea
between the floundering ship and the reef.

I was momentarily in the jaws of death. But
one comforting thing remained with me. I heard
the familiar words and now identified the voice,
"He's gone! He's gone!" The captain flashed his
light and saw me disappear under water. He
thought I was lost. He jumped ashore to see if he
could help me, but in the confusion which fol-

lowed we had become separated. As one wave receded, my head broke water and I gasped for air and clawed wildly for what is normally shunned —the razor-sharp coral reef covered with poisonous fungus film. I grasped the slimly reef and held on firmly as the receding surf sucked about me, nearly dislodging me and swirling me under the ship.

The thought of being crushed to death was very real to me now, for the ship had been steadily crushing itself to death at this very spot. I could not understand why the ship did not crash down upon me. I was prepared to die. It seemed an eternity before I could move. Suddenly I felt the pressure of suction released. I knew I had but a few seconds to lift my body up over the reef or risk being ripped to pieces by the sharp coral fingers all about me when the next wave hit.

Divine Providence

What happened in the next few minutes I must credit to divine providence, for no one could have come out of such a desperate situation without a bruise, although my clothes were torn to shreds. When I came to myself out of a mild state of shock I found myself being bumped intermittently by floating objects from the ship, but I was now in shallow water and had firm footing. I raised my eyes heavenward and in audible words thanked my heavenly Father with a smile on my lips for a testimony of his power toward me, one of his weakest and most unworthy servants.

A hideous crash reminded me that we were still in danger. What had happened to the others? I ran back toward the disaster area and met the captain, who flung his arms around me and in tears stated that he had thought I was killed in the accident. We both ran toward the edge of the reef and called to the others. They were now in the lifeboat some distance offshore, but the ship had been heaved upon the reef by the force of the waves and it now lay groaning and creaking as the force of the waves inched it up on the shelf of the reef.

The passengers, one of them a Catholic, stated that when I jumped ashore the ship was pushed away from the shore against the waves as if by a giant hand. The ship then righted itself for the first time long enough for them to get the lifeboat down. As soon as they were in the boat, the ship was carried quickly back and crushed on the reef.

This is the meaning of a shipwreck in the dangerous archipelago. I can underscore the words of Paul, who said, "And now I exhort you to be of good cheer: for there shall be no loss of any man's life among you, but of the ship. For there stood by me this night the angel of God, whose I am and whom I serve . . ."

Chapter 19

Monument to Captain Cook

Mutiny on the Bounty

One of the men responsible for the immortalizing of the "Bounty" incident lived but a few kilometers from our mission headquarters at Papeete, Tahiti. James Norman Hall, one of the noted authors of our time and a warm personal friend, invited me to his home at Arue, Tahiti.

One beautiful tropical morning I left Papeete by bicycle via the Macadamized Route de Ceinture and headed toward the Bay of Matavai where once the colorful ships of Captain Bligh lay at anchor.

It took about thirty minutes to make the trip which allowed for frequent rest stops and time to explore the beaches at the most inviting points of interest. When I finally arrived at Mr. Hall's home, I leaned my bicycle against the side of the house and walked up on the veranda. I rapped gently on the door post. Everything was so quiet and peaceful the hollow knock brought a quick stir from within. Mr. Hall, a pleasant man of medium build, soon appeared at the door and invited me to enter. He led me into his den in an adjoining room.

The house was beautifully arranged with true Polynesian decor. He asked me to be seated in a Polynesian chair placed directly in front of his work desk. He sat down behind his typewriter and we were soon deep in conversation. His hair, graying at the temples, made his dark eyebrows seem to stand out unnaturally. His neatly trimmed mustache showed streaks of gray. His eyes seemed to twinkle as we talked of matters of mutual concern.

The Far Lands

We discussed his latest book *The Far Lands* which describes the most ancient migrations from Asia to the islands of the sea. He pointed out that the bulk of modern science seems to support this theory of origin for Polynesia from Asia which contrasts sharply with the Kon-Tiki theory of origin from ancient America.

This was a natural point for me to interject a thought about the Book of Mormon. I presented Mr. Hall a specially marked copy of the Book of Mormon and called to his attention that it was an ancient record written by early voyagers in the Pacific. He was surprised to learn that it suggested both the Asian and American theories of Polynesian origin. We covered the field too hurriedly to do justice to the subject, but the markings I had made in the book before visiting Mr. Hall were from the standpoint of a study in anthropology relating to the American aborigines.

He seemed genuinely interested in the message of the Book of Mormon and promised to pursue the subject further in his moments of leisure. He placed the book in his library, and in exchange took a copy of *The Far Lands* and presented it to me as a personal gift. The book deals with Polynesian migrations into the Pacific in the primordial past. In the front he wrote, "For Edward Butterworth with best wishes from James Norman Hall, Arue', Tahiti, March 24th, 1951."

We did not talk much of religion, but it was he who turned the conversation to that subject as he spoke of his respect for missionaries and religion in general, while lamenting the fact that he had not taken religion more seriously himself. He spoke affectionately of his actor son, Conrad, who was at the time working with Walt Disney on the Hollywood movie, "The Living Desert."

The "Bounty" Incident

Mr. Hall suggested that we seek a cooler atmosphere for our remaining conversation. We left the house to stroll around the green velvet lawn in front of his home. He dispatched a servant for refreshments, and when they were brought, we sat down in the shade of a large tree near his front door.

It was an impressive sight from our vantage point. The coral lagoon lay directly before us, quiet except for the washboard ripples at the very edge as they charged up in a white foam and disappeared magically into the black sand. A few rods farther away a delicate silken spray was occasionally thrown up by the breakers as they rolled incessantly over the fringing reef; and beyond that, of course, was the endless sea.

The faint roar of tumbling waters seemed to set the stage for some inspiring pageant which was about to begin. Actually the pageant had made its strophe and antistrophe many decades earlier across this very stage. It would have faded into oblivion except for this imaginative genius in whose presence I now sat.

"Nearly two hundred years ago," Mr. Hall began with a gesture toward the lagoon, "Captain Bligh dropped the Bounty's anchor in this very bay."

I admitted that I did not recall the details of the "Bounty" story, so Mr. Hall obligingly recounted some of the more important but little known incidents connected with that colorful saga.

He Tells the Story

"Lieutenant William Bligh," Mr. Hall continued, "had been sailing master for four years under the great navigator, Captain Cook, who sailed the famous ship, 'The Resolution.' In 1787, about the month of August, Lieutenant Bligh was appointed commander and purser of the 'Bounty' and his rank was advanced to captain. The ship was stored and victualed for eighteen months, with such supplies as portable soup, essence of meat, sauerkraut, and dried malt. They also added trading stores, such as iron articles, steel, trinkets, beads, looking glasses, and other items, to traffic with the natives. The purpose of the trip was to collect plants of the breadfruit variety in order to convey them to the West Indies to supply the growing demands for food among the slaves there.

"Sir Joseph Banks had visited Tahiti with Captain Cook in 1769, and upon seeing the tremendous

James Norman Hall, author of "Mutiny on the Bounty," in his office

amount of food supplied by this remarkable tree he reported to the authorities in England that it could be successfully cultivated in the climate of the West Indies.

"The 'Bounty' was fitted out at Deptford, England, under the supervision of Captain Bligh himself. A false floor had been made to fit over the floor of the great cabin in which holes had been cut to contain the garden pots into which the plants were to be carefully placed.

"The 'Bounty' was a ship of about 215 tons burden, and when it left Spithead on the twenty-third of December, 1787, it had forty-six people on board including the captain and his crew. The voyage to Tahiti was attended with many circumstances and difficulties and dangers unlimited. We tried to preserve the details of that memorable journey in our Book *Mutiny on the Bounty.*

"She dropped anchor here in Matavai Bay in the forenoon of October 26, 1788, at ten o'clock. The details of the sojourn of the 'Bounty' is the burden of the book and much too long to recount at the present time. Suffice it to say, they collected 1,105 plants and carefully transplanted them in the pots arranged in the false floor of the great cabin. They collected other plants, too, but these were incidental. When Mr. Christian finally called for the mutiny to begin, the 'Bounty' had left Tahiti and reached the Friendly Islands at Tofoa. Twenty-five of the original seamen followed Mr. Fletcher Christian, and eighteen followed Captain Bligh. Those loyal to Bligh were put adrift at sea in the ship's launch, ostensibly to perish, but due to the miraculous turn of events and the hardy nature of the seamen they somehow survived the ordeal. The story of that hardy band of men is told in another narrative, *Men against the Sea.*

"The mutineers steered the 'Bounty' back to this bay and took many natives, men and women, with them and sailed away to Pitcairn Island. This is, very briefly, the history of the *Mutiny on the Bounty,*" Mr. Hall concluded.

"There is a complete set of your books at the Museum," I said, "and I will certainly read them as soon as I can find time." This was a promise I was pleased to keep; in fact after having begun to read, I was so interested in the books I read one of them three times.

"Mr. Hall," I said with sincere appreciation, "I don't know when I have spent a more enjoyable time with anyone. I really cannot thank you enough for giving me so much of your valuable time."

"I'm always glad to take time out to converse with a friend," he said generously.

I needed to get back to Tarona, so I took my reluctant leave of this great man and cycled back. He had invited me to bring my wife for a social evening after my return from the Marquesas.

Sad News

Unfortunately this was an appointment we were never privileged to keep. Very shortly after this visit to the home of James Norman Hall, I was far out to sea on board the government schooner "Te Orophena," heading toward the Marquesas when the news of his death was broadcast over Radio Tahiti in the Polynesian language. His book *Mutiny on the Bounty* was under my soiled pillow at that very moment, and his latest book, *The Far Lands,* was in my brief case. I took out the books and exhibited them to the sailors on "Te Orophena" and told them of my latest visit with him. I proudly pointed to the autograph which Mr. Hall had recorded in the front of my book. I am reasonably sure this is the last book he ever autographed. It was a sad evening for us all, for another romantic era had closed and another brilliant light had flickered and gone out.

Chapter 20

*F. Edward Butterworth in front of
the church at Papeete*

The First Missionaries

Ancient Tahiti produced some of the world's most docile and pleasant aboriginal peoples; yet savagery and even human sacrifice were not unknown among them on some of the most primitive and isolated islands as late as the nineteenth century. Many people erroneously confuse Hawaii and Tahiti, believing them to be the same group of Pacific Islands. It is true that the inhabitants of these widely separated islands are related, but it is important that we recognize the distinct differences between them in order to comprehend their true significance in church history.

Polynesia

The Greek term "Poly-nesia" (many islands) adequately describes the area of the Pacific where these people were discovered in A.D. 1765. A triangle drawn from Hawaii to New Zealand and Easter Island includes nearly all of Polynesia. Tahiti, the hub of Polynesia as it falls near the center of this triangle, was the original home of the Maori and Hawaiian natives. The aborigines of New Zealand are called "Maori"; in Hawaii, "Hawaiian"; and in Tahiti, "Tahitian." The proper pronunciation of "Tahitian" employs four syllables—"Tä-hē'-tē-àn," although the more common pronunciation is the familiar three-syllable "Ta-hish'-àn."

The area of Polynesia where our church has been established is called "French Polynesia," as it fell under the domination of the French in 1843. The main divisions of French Polynesia where our church work is established are the Society Islands, with branches on Tahiti, Moorea, and Makatea; the Austral Islands, on Tubuai; the Tuamotuan Islands, where the bulk of our membership lives; and the islands to the west which are presently being considered for missionary expansion. If we refer to our South Sea Island Mission as the "Society Islands," we do not include the bulk of our members who live outside the Society Islands. It is more accurate to refer to this mission as French Polynesia.

Our Missionaries Arrive

The French were in the process of subduing Tahiti when our first missionaries, Seventies Noah Rogers and Benjamin F. Grouard, sailed into the harbor on board the ship "Timoleon" May 14, 1844. Noah Rogers was French Polynesia's first mission president, although his contribution to the islands should not overshadow the ministry of the unsung hero, Benjamin F. Grouard. Seventy Knowlton Hanks, also assigned by Joseph Smith, Jr., to ministry in the islands, was buried at sea before arriving. Seventy Addison Pratt made his worthy contribution on Tubuai in the Austral Islands. Without detracting from the sacrifices and successful ministry of Addison Pratt, we must, in all honesty, take into consideration the fact that his ministry was unimpaired by

200

war and the competition of other faiths. It is true that he made the first converts to the faith, but again we must take into account the fact that he had the advantage of several months before Benjamin F. Grouard and Noah Rogers were allowed to preach in public on Tahiti.

Benjamin F. Grouard

Noah Rogers spent much of his time while in the islands doing missionary work in the Protestant-held Western Islands. He met with severe missionary opposition in these areas and after fourteen months decided to return to America, with few notable results of his missionary work in the South Sea Islands. Addison Pratt remained in the islands a year and eight months and firmly established the work on Tubuai; then he, too, returned to America, leaving Benjamin Grouard to handle the mission alone.

At Papeete, Brother Grouard boarded with one of the passengers of the "Timoleon," Seth Lincoln, with whom he had become acquainted during their long journey to Polynesia. After a few weeks Mr. Lincoln was baptized and ordained. He became the first branch president at Papeete, Tahiti.

Despite the difficulties encountered on Tahiti, some fifteen or twenty members were gathered into the Restoration in the first few months of Elders Grouard and Rogers' ministry. All of these were American and English, as the natives feared the wrath of the English Protestants, through whom they expected to receive help from England in their

*Monument to
Addison Pratt*

skirmishes with the French. Realizing that he would have greater success in the outer islands, Brother Grouard left the mission work on Tahiti in charge of Brother Lincoln and joined Addison Pratt on Tubuai for a period of one month. He returned to Tahiti for two months, then sailed by trading schooner for Anaa, one of the Tuamotuan Chain Islands, where he made his most notable contribution.

A Savage Island Tamed

It was well known to everyone acquainted with French Polynesia that Anaa was occupied by the most feared and savage natives in the Tuamotu. It is quite possible, however, that Brother Grouard did not know this; but if he did, he should be considered one of the most fearless missionaries the Restoration has ever known. He writes of his arrival: "As we drew near the land I noticed that the beach was already lined with natives awaiting our arrival, and as we came nearer, I could distinctly hear them shout and jabber like a flock of ten thousand wild geese. I can hardly describe my feelings as I approached this strange land and heard the wild shouts of these half-civilized sons of the ocean. It seemed as if I had left the world and got upon another planet, among another class of beings. They were certainly a different race of people from any I had hitherto seen. My time for meditation, however, was short, for we soon arrived at the landing place, and leaping ashore, I found myself the next minute surrounded by some two or three hundred natives of both sexes and all ages; naked, half-naked, and dressed; hooting, hallooing, laughing, and jabbering like a legion of evil spirits. In my eyes they looked wild and savage-like; I listened to their frightful noises, and not being able to understand what they said, I knew not but what I had become a victim for a sacrifice in very deed."

Brother Grouard remained on this island, fired with a zeal to promulgate the gospel despite the anxiety which gripped him upon his arrival. He was able to baptize six natives during his first month among them, and after four months and twenty-one days he had baptized six hundred and twenty persons, ordained seventeen priesthood members, and organized five branches of the Restoration. One of the greatest chapters of missionary accomplishment the Restoration has known was written in the hearts of these savage inhabitants of Anaa, Tuamotu.

After Addison Pratt's departure for America in December, 1845, Benjamin F. Grouard carried on the missionary work alone for three years. He built his own thirty-foot vessel of sawn plank, without a piece of iron or a nail in the entire construction. His vessel was demolished on the reef at Mehetia. He was forced to build another, but in the process of building, he was able to baptize two more converts to the faith. Brother Grouard traveled alone in these small vessels from island to island and succeeded in holding the church together at the very time the church in America was being scattered by persecution and apostasy.

Pratt Returns from America

It may have been the stigma of strange doctrine brought back from America in 1850 by Addison Pratt and James Brown which resulted in their confinement to prison at Papeete, although there is no evidence that Addison Pratt ever taught polygamy in the islands. It is true, nevertheless, that both he and his traveling companion, James Brown, were confined to prison for several months for preaching Mormonism. Sometime after Pratt's release from prison and the stipulation that he not visit the outer

Marker honoring the site of first church, erected under direction of Addison Pratt

islands was lifted, he joined Brother Grouard at Tubuai in the Australs. For two years they labored together in that area.

It must have been very discouraging indeed to Brother Grouard to learn of the death of the prophet, Joseph Smith, Jr., and the usurpation of leadership by Brigham Young. He never quite recovered from the shock. In 1852 both Pratt and Grouard returned to America, leaving the work in the care of Elder John Hawkins.

Brother Grouard refused to follow the leadership of Brigham Young and subsequently left the church to become associated with spiritualism. He died outside the faith at Santa Ana, California, in 1894.

Addison Pratt also showed signs of disillusionment and died estranged from Brigham Young and from his own wife, who was a rabid follower of Young, and exponent of doctrines opposed by Addison Pratt. In her diary, Mrs. Pratt writes concerning her husband, "Differences of opinion sometimes rose between us in regard to certain principles which had been revealed in his absence." Addison Pratt did not approve of dancing, nor would he allow it in the islands. The fact that he did not accept polygamy, condone dancing, nor support Brigham Young in his opposition to the U. S. Government implies that these were evidently the principles revealed during his absence with which he was not in sympathy. It is singular to note that neither Grouard nor Pratt would settle in Salt Lake City.

John Hawkins

Elder John Hawkins was converted, baptized, and ordained by Seventy Benjamin F. Grouard in 1844 at Tiona. He was an Englishman who became thoroughly converted to the faith. He was largely responsible for holding our few people in the nearby islands steadfast to the faith during the many years when no foreign ministry could enter the islands. He rejected requests from ministers of certain factions of the Restoration who, upon passing Tahiti en route to America, desired an audience at Tiona. It is said one of his reasons for rejecting them was the fact that they condoned polygamy. Upon the arrival of Elders Glaud Rodger and Charles Wandell of the Reorganization, the natives felt the kindred spirit of the original organization and permitted these good brethren to reorganize the church at Tiona.

Persecution in the Islands

After the missionaries were deported in 1852, the Saints were subjected to bitter persecution. An experience on the island of Anaa is an extreme example of persecution suffered by the Saints during the years 1853-1872. No "stranger" missionaries were allowed to enter Tahiti during this period, which gave the Catholic church a free hand in the conversion of the natives by force.

One Sunday morning the Saints were gathered for worship, as was their custom, in a small coconut thatch meeting house on the island of Anaa. During the service a French gendarme, reportedly under the influence of liquor, carelessly and disrespectfully entered the building brandishing his sword and demanding the immediate cessation of their so-called heretical worship. He was followed into the church by two Catholic priests. One elderly woman refused to rise from her attitude of prayer. The gendarme raised his sword to strike her, but it caught momentarily in the low thatch roofing. This slight hesitation was a mortal miscalculation on his part. The natives on Anaa carried their fishing spears to church and not being too far removed from savagery were quick to fight back, recognizing this grave injustice to one of their own kind. Needless to say, the gendarme was killed on the spot with spears and clubs, and one of the priests (Caret) also met death at that time. The second priest (Laval) carried a deep sword wound across his face

New mission house at Tarona (Papeete,
Tahiti). Church spire is seen
behind the house

as a grim reminder of this encounter on the savage
island of Anaa.

Hostages and Prisoners

This unfortunate incident aroused the entire
officialdom of French Polynesia against the defense-
less Saints. The island of Anaa soon swarmed with
military and penal officers. The men who had actually attacked the intruding officer and priests took
refuge in the cave "Tefaitiga," which is entered by
a secret passage below the surface of the water.
Failing to find the accused men, the officials selected
five hostages and hanged them in public. Mapeura,
a deep-sea diver, had to be hanged three times be-

fore he finally succumbed to this cruel execution. One hundred and twenty-seven prisoners from Anaa were taken to Papeete as a result of this accusation against them and made to work on a road construction program. They were marched to church at the point of a bayonet, and only fifteen of the one hundred and twenty-seven lived to return to their native Anaa.

Disorganization

Except for the few faithful souls at Tiona, Kaukura, and Makatea, the early church members broke up into factions as a result of the pressure of persecution and lack of leadership. Many went into the Catholic church to escape persecution; others changed their name to "Israelites," probably for the same reason; and still others just drifted about, claiming to be followers of Grouard, but rejecting the Doctrine and Covenants and all teachings not mentioned by Grouard. The headquarters of the faithful was set up at Tiona (Zion), a few miles from Papeete.

This brings to a close the history in brief of the original church in French Polynesia, and closes one of the most colorful chapters of missionary work connected with the Restoration.

Chapter 21

Polynesian children with Missionary Butterworth. He calls them the "hope of the mission."

The Church Returns

The original church, now reorganized, entered Tahiti about twenty years ahead of all factions of the Restoration. From 1852 until 1870 no entry permits for "stranger" missionaries were issued by the French. It was indeed a singular manner in which the Lord moved to re-establish his church in the South Sea Islands.

Glaud Rodger and Charles Wandell

On December 13, 1873, Elder John Hawkins was away on the island of Kaukura when the frail bark "Domingo" (Sunday), which carried Glaud Rodger and Charles Wandell, put in at Papeete for repairs. They were en route to Australia to open up the work in that place when their ship sprang a leak, threatening their safety and forcing them to change their course for Tahiti. This permitted a visit of approximately two weeks by the missionaries without the restrictions of entry visas.

Unfortunately, however, they did not locate the lonely Saints at "Tiona" until two or three days before their departure. They were the first missionaries of the church to contact these people since the 1852 deportation of Seventies B. F. Grouard and Addison Pratt, although during this interim some representatives of the Mormon church on their way to America from Australia had contacted the Saints. In open conference, however, the native Saints rejected the doctrine of polygamy and consequently the faction which attempted to introduce it.

Tiona

In the absence of missionary John Hawkins, whom Brethren Grouard and Pratt had left in charge twenty years earlier, the local presiding elder, Brother David Brown, received Elders Rodger and Wandell at Tiona. Brother Brown explained that the native Saints had gathered at Tiona to withdraw from the wicked city of Papeete and to keep the children out of the Catholic schools. A police officer explained to the visiting missionaries that another reason for their withdrawal to Tiona was to escape religious persecution. The Saints had their own bamboo church building at Tiona with a bell to call them to service. They held regular meetings three times each Sunday with a Communion service once each month. According to the diary of Mrs. Addison Pratt, it was evidently Addison Pratt who introduced the once-a-month practice of serving the Communion. Quarterly conferences were held for the entire faithful membership, which was estimated to be around five hundred in number.

The Departure of the Missionaries

On Sunday, December 21, 1873, a memorable day in the course of the history of the islands, Brother Glaud Rodger baptized fifty-one persons. Government or religious spies among them carried this information to the authorities, and the missionaries were accosted twice and charged with an infraction of the French law. Upon their arrival at Papeete, however, they were permitted to depart without difficulty. The luscious feast, the haunting rhythmical songs, and the tearful parting described by Brother Wandell are typically Polynesian.

The missionaries left Papeete on Christmas Day, 1873, elated by the pleasant memories of a good work accomplished in the South Sea Islands. They had been instrumental in introducing the Reorganization of the original Latter Day Saint Church in Polynesia.

William Nelson

On July 23, 1878, five years after Brother Wandell had requested missionary help for the islands, Brother William Nelson arrived at Papeete. He baptized thirty people his first three months in the islands and organized the work at Papeete and in the Tuamotu and was the first minister of the Reorganization to visit the outer islands. He returned to America in 1883 after performing a wonderful holding ministry.

Apostle T. W. Smith

Apostle T. W. Smith arrived at Papeete on November 6, 1884, the first Apostle of the Restoration to enter French Polynesia. He will long be remembered for his powerful preaching, the quality of his

*A group of priesthood at a local
district conference*

ministry, and the printing of tracts, laws, and short
suggested prayers dealing with the ordinances.

It was during the ministry of Apostle T. W.
Smith that the headquarters of the church was
moved from Tiona to Papeete. A piece of waste-
land in the section of town called Fareute was donated by a good native sister, Tariirii a Vehiatua.
Later the adjoining properties were accumulated by
purchase and subsequently developed into our present beautiful compound called "Tarona."

Tidal Wave of 1903

Following Brother T. W. Smith, such well-known
ministers as Luther Devore, William Newton, Mark
Forscutt, and J. W. Gilbert crossed the panorama
of island history. Of these brethren, Brother Gilbert is the best known among the islanders. This
was partly due to his unexcelled contribution to the

islands during the tidal wave of 1903, when hundreds of our people were killed and several of our churches demolished. He is best known for his improvisation of a condenser to render pure the saline surf which had drowned the island of Hikueru. The survivors were saved by this ingenious device. Frequent tribute is paid to Brother Gilbert.

"Te Evanelia"

The frail ship "Te Evanelia" (The Gospel) was launched September 14, 1894, and dedicated September 23 in the presence of two hundred Saints in the San Francisco area. A veteran sea captain, Elder Joseph Burton, was selected by the General Conference to pilot "Te Evanelia" to Tahiti. The details of this journey were recorded in the book *Beatrice Witherspoon,* written by Sister Burton.

Brother and Sister Hubert Case were the first missionaries of the Reorganization to attempt to establish the Reorganized Church in the Cook Islands. They are best remembered, however, for their good work on the island of Hikueru.

"Te Evanelia" was not used long for missionary work as had been originally intended, due to the unforeseen difficulties of French ownership and restrictions on foreign captains. The ship was finally made into a copra schooner, but on July 18, 1896, it met disaster at sea and sank between the islands of Tikehau and Rairoa. The nine passengers aboard at the time were picked up by a small boat "Teumere" from the island of Rairoa.

Alexander Smith in the Islands

Elder J. W. Peterson succeeded Brother Burton as mission president and was instrumental in getting a native brother, Elder "Metuaore," to visit the General Conference in America. Elder Metuaore is the only native in the history of the mission to be ordained to the office of Bishop. President Alexander Smith accompanied Elder Metuaore and two other missionary families (the Burtons and Gilberts) to Tahiti following the General Conference and ordained him in the islands. Alexander Smith was the first member of the First Presidency to visit Tahiti. As a patriarch, too, he was able to perform a double ministry in the islands.

Doctrine and Covenants Translated

During the ministry of Brethren Joseph Burton and J. W. Gilbert, the native Doctrine and Covenants was a result of the translation by Mr. Isaac Henry and printed at Tahiti. About one thousand copies were distributed. These have been lost, worn out, or guarded so carefully that only a few can be located in the entire mission.

General Church Officers Who Have Visited Tahiti

FIRST PRESIDENCY
I. A. Smith (1950)
Alexander Smith (1900)
F. Henry Edwards (1954)

BISHOPS
A. V. Karlstrom (1919)
Mark Siegfried (1950)

APOSTLES
T. W. Smith (1894)
Gomer Griffiths (1913)
Paul Hanson (1915)
John Rushton (1919)
C. F. Ellis (1924)
G. G. Lewis (1934)
C. G. Mesley (1946)
C. R. Hield (1954)
Reed M. Holmes (1960)

216

PATRIARCHS
A. H. Smith (1900)
F. G. Pitt (1913)
J. C. May (1951)

Mission Presidents Since 1900

Joseph Burton
Charles Lake
J. Charles May
C. F. Ellis

Robert Brown
Hinman Savage
R. J. Farthing
Joseph Yager

F. Edward Butterworth
V. C. Sorensen
A. J. Breckenridge
Alan D. Tyree

Present Church Status in French Polynesia

The Reorganized Church of Jesus Christ of Latter Day Saints ranks third among the religions of Tahiti. For the purpose of comparison we here reprint an excerpt from the 1951 religious census of French Polynesia:

	Prot.	Cath.	R.L.D.S.	Mor.	7th. Day Adv.	Non-Dec.
Tahiti and Dependencies	19,377	7,804	597	480	385	6 780
Western Islands	10,745	446	—	10	327	1,392
Marquesas	387	2,773	16	—	1	80
Australs	3,422	135	114	218	75	19
Tuamotu	494	3,443	1,346	510	6	767
Gambiers	16	495	—	—	—	—
Totals	34,441	15,096	2,073*	1,218	794	9,039

*Our own statistics show about 2,300 members in the mission.